SOULTALK

SOULTALK

Speaking with Power into the Lives of Others

DR. LARRY CRABB

THOMAS NELSON
Since 1798

NASHVILLE   DALLAS   MEXICO CITY   RIO DE JANEIRO   BEIJING

Published in Nashville, Tennessee, by Thomas Nelson. Thomas Nelson is a trademark of Thomas Nelson, Inc.

Thomas Nelson, Inc. titles may be purchased in bulk for educational, business, fund-raising, or sales promotional use. For information, please e-mail SpecialMarkets@ThomasNelson.com.

Published in association with Yates & Yates, LLP,
Attorneys and Counselors, Orange, California

Cover Design: UDG | Designworks
Interior: Inside Out Design & Typesetting

Library of Congress Cataloging-in-Publication Data

Crabb, Lawrence J.
Soultalk : speaking with power into the lives of others / by Larry Crabb.
p. cm.

ISBN 10: 1-59145-039-X (hc)
ISBN 13: 978-1-59145-039-9 (hc)
ISBN 10: 1-59145-347-X (tp)
ISBN 13: 978-1-59145-347-5 (tp)

1. Spiritual life—Christianity.   I. Title: Soul talk.   II. Title.
BV4501.3C735   2003
248.4–dc22   2003014233

Printed in the United States of America
07 08 09 10 RRD 9 8 7 6 5

To our Intentional Spiritual Formation Group:

Thanks for the opportunity you provide for each of us

to learn the language

God longs for us to speak.

CONTENTS

ACKNOWLEDGMENTS

WITHOUT JOEY PAUL, this book would not have been written. Thanks, Joey, and thanks to Byron, Rob, Kris, Jennifer, and the entire Integrity team.

Sealy, your encouragement and guidance means a lot. Thanks for your commitment to kingdom work.

Friendships deepen when SoulTalk is spoken. Trip, our conversations are literally life-giving. Evan, your heart is anchored in first things; that strengthens my faith. Dwight, Jimmy, and Kent, you help me see that the narrow path is inviting. Bob and Claudia, your investment in me has made my soul rich. Thank you all, and many more.

To all who have spent a week with me in our School of Spiritual Direction: You've given me the awesome privilege of watching the Spirit work right in front of my eyes. Amazing! Thank you.

Family provides the richest tastes of real life, and those tastes energize me to write. Kim and Lesley, I count you both among my most celebrated blessings. Josie, Jake, and Kaitlyn, I hope you hear lots of SoulTalk from Pop-Pop. Kep and Ken, I can't write your names without tearing up. You believe in me and my calling. And Rachael, we walk together—I have no greater joy on earth.

Mom and Dad, if you're listening: Thanks for everything! See you soon.

INTRODUCTION

When Life Begins

SHORTLY AFTER NOON on July 5, 1997, the doctor told me I had cancer. I can't recall the physician's name, but I can see his face as clearly as if I were watching a video of him walking into my hospital room, where my wife and I awaited his diagnosis. I see the thick, dark moustache draped over a full mouth and the intense Hispanic eyes looking at me with kind sadness, which I instantly registered with alarm.

He stood at the foot of my bed, the way a nervous missionary might keep his distance from a leper. I sensed he wanted to come closer, maybe touch my shoulder, but he remained at a professional distance while he spoke.

And I can still hear his voice as distinctly as if he were speaking to me right now. His accent was pronounced, almost as thick as his moustache, but I had absolutely no trouble making out every word. "We just got the results from your

CAT scan. You have a mass the size of a tennis ball near your stomach. We're pretty certain it's malignant."

My wife and I cried when the doctor left. He had made no promises. We didn't know if I'd live or die.

Most of us live for years determined not to look too closely into our soul.

It takes awhile to realize what life is all about. We don't ask the hard questions until we have to. That day, I had to. The doctor's words got me thinking, more than I had since my brother was killed six years earlier in a plane crash, about what I'm doing here, how I'm supposed to maneuver through life's unpredictability, what I really want out of life, and whether it's available.

The curtains covering my soul fell back, and I began to see what was happening inside. When that occurred, the battle began. But it's also when *life* began.

SEEING INSIDE OUR SOUL

Most of us live for years determined not to look too closely into our soul. We don't want to get that well acquainted with ourselves and with the world we live in. We worry that if we looked closely at what we want and what's available, if we saw all that was happening in our soul, we'd give up or go mad or maybe become religious fanatics, nut cases for Jesus who hold up John 3:16 placards at football games—or maybe worse.

But that's not what happens when we see all the way inside. That's not what takes place when we catch a clear glimpse of the real inside story. It's a partial look that does the damage.

look for the sun-rise in our Soul

A full search into our own soul causes life to begin, not end. And then it's as if we've never lived before. Dark nights may not go away, but they hold the promise of a bright morning. This world's sunsets become another world's sunrises. And joy comes into sight.

But not right away. Our eyes, so used to artificial light, take awhile to adjust to the sunlight. We're no longer sure if we've ever seen the sun and felt its warmth or if we'll ever see it and feel it again. Darkness can seem like the end of our final day.

REDISCOVERING A DESIRE FOR GOD

My wife, Rachael, had to leave at eight o'clock that evening— hospital rules. Surgery was scheduled for first thing Tuesday morning, July 8. I lay in bed for about an hour and then got up, checked my hospital gown to make sure it was tied in the back, and walked to the window. I was on the ninth floor in St. Joseph's Hospital in downtown Denver. It was Saturday night.

I looked down and saw dozens of cars, each one crawling steadily along crisscrossing streets like insects in a maze searching for food. One street was bordered by a neon-lit nightspot with a huge sign flashing "Booze and Broads." The corner to the left featured a closed-for-the-night Einstein's Bagels shop facing east and a still-open Starbucks facing north. A medical office building with one lighted window towered above two one-story buildings in need of paint: one a dry cleaning business, the other a restaurant, each with the same Chinese name.

When truth is hard to face, you notice unimportant facts;

then fantasy kicks in to help you look at things. I imagined a happily married couple, about Rachael's and my age, in one of the cars, on their way home from a pleasant evening at the Denver Performing Arts Center. I wondered which play they had seen at which theater. When the car I was watching pulled into Starbucks, I pictured them as a Christian married couple, deciding on a nightcap of decaf lattes and one lemon bar to split before they drove home, snuggled together, then got up early the next morning for the Sunday paper and church.

I remember thinking, *They have the abundant life. I have cancer. It's not fair. I'm up here in a hospital room, by myself. My wife is home crying herself to sleep, praying to a God who gives no guarantees, and I've got a tennis ball–sized cyst inside me that could end my life. And they're having a good time. That's what I want!*

Trusting thoughts don't come easily at times like that. Silly thoughts do. Like this one: *Maybe it's because I skipped devotions on Friday that I was diagnosed with cancer on Saturday. If I have devotions, long ones, and memorize a few verses tomorrow and the next day, then when they open me up on Tuesday, maybe they'll see that the tennis ball is a harmless, easily removed cyst, cut it out, sew me up, and send me home.*

When you try to explain the unexplainable in an effort to control the uncontrollable, every thought is silly. And every emotion is confused and unstable.

I could feel a haughty arrogance sweep through me ("I don't deserve this!") and give way to despair ("I can't handle this!"), and then the arrogance roared back with obvious anger ("Who's doing this to me?"). Then resignation settled in, a *Who cares?*

attitude I tried to pretend was peace. Then more confusion ("I just don't get it.").

But then, for reasons that lie in a realm beyond reason, I could feel my thoughts drifting. I suddenly had the image in my mind of the devil approaching Jesus for a chat. Still looking out the window of my high-up hospital room, I rehearsed the gist of their conversation from memory.

Satan spoke first. "I've got a plan, Jesus, a wonderful plan for your life. It's certainly a lot better than the one you've been already assigned. You *do* know what's ahead, don't you, if you don't change course? Instant popularity that will quickly fade and leave you a hated, has-been Messiah; powerful enemies who will turn your cheering fans into an angry mob that will scream for your life; friends who will fall asleep when you need them most; a close buddy who will give you up to save his own skin; and a death worse than you could ever imagine. Jesus, that *can't* be what you want. You can do so much better than that. Interested?

"For starters, fix yourself a meal. You can do it. Take control! Use your power! You *are* hungry, aren't you? What's wrong with satisfying a normal desire? C'mon, you'll feel better.

"Look down and see the streets of every city in the world. Theaters, coffee shops, nice homes, places of worship, golf courses, art museums—you can have it all. It's all mine to give. I'll put you in charge; you call all the shots, have whatever you want. You can be a winner!

"And I'll make you more popular than you've ever dreamed.

You need a platform to get your message out, don't you? I've got a marketing plan that will put your picture on the front page of every paper in print. You'll be on *Oprah, Larry King Live,* and *20/20.*

"Here's the deal. I have the resources to supply everything you could possibly want in this world. And I'll do it. But you have to cooperate. It won't take much. All you have to do is turn to your Father and say, 'I really love you and want to be close to you, but I want these things more.' That's it! That's all you have to do. Don't even mention my name if you don't want to. Do it for yourself!"

I was still looking down at Starbucks. I could see the couple sitting by the window, sipping coffee and chatting. I thought about Jesus' response. "I will exercise my power to do only one thing, and that is to stay close to my Father, to do whatever he wants me to do. When the choice is between legitimate pleasures of life and intimacy with my Father, there is no choice. I'd rather have him and nothing else than everything without him. Pleasure at the expense of his delight in me would be no pleasure at all. It is the only pain I could not bear. Satan, your words have no appeal. Leave!"

I then left my post by the window, lay down in bed, and reflected. I could feel my mind still carried along like a little boat in a steady current. A parable told by Saint Augustine two thousand years earlier floated into my mind. I remembered it like this:

Suppose, Augustine said, God himself came to you and invited you to draw up your ultimate wish list, with things on it we'd all agree are OK for Jesus followers to enjoy: a good meal when you're hungry, great family life, a satisfying sense of purpose and meaning, the excitement of romance and adventure, robust health, a job that showcases your unique talents and earns you respect and lots of money, a season pass to the theater or to the ski slopes, a good night's sleep every night on your dial-a-number mattress, and, to top it off nicely, a good experience in church Sunday mornings where you gratefully worship the generous God who gave it all to you.

Suppose also that while you're looking over your list and deciding it's pretty complete—you might throw in a new car, maybe a boat and a vacation home—God speaks again. This time he says, "I will give you everything on your list, and I will grant you a long life to enjoy it all. But there is a condition, only one: If you accept this offer, *you will never see my face!*"

Augustine explained his parable this way: "The chill that you feel when you think of never seeing God's face is your love for God." As those words came to mind, directed, I now realize, by God's Spirit, I cried. They were tears of illumination, tears of hope and joy.

Of course I wanted to be healthy. Of course I would rather sip lattes with my wife in Starbucks than drink water by myself from a plastic cup in St. Joseph's room 917. I'm no masochist. I don't *like* to suffer.

But I understood. For a moment it was clear. *Life is all about knowing God!* It's all about him, and because he loves us, it's all about him and me, him and you, you and me in him. Knowing him is what I want more than anything. And knowing the Father is what Jesus makes possible for me!

I understood something else. My biggest problem was how out of touch I had been—and would be again—with my desire for God. I was more aware of my desires for health and good times with Rachael.

 That night the cobwebs cleared, and my eyes focused. I could see into my soul—and I realized that I wanted God more than anything or anyone else, with my whole being. That was the first miracle.

Then came the second miracle, even better than the first. No, the tennis ball–sized cyst didn't suddenly disappear. Surgery was still coming. But a strange peace came over me. I felt joy. Yet even the peace and joy weren't really the point. *That night I experienced the* *presence of God.* What more—or less—could I want?

I realized then what I now want everyone to know—that every hard thing we endure can put us in touch with our desire for God, and every trial can strengthen that desire until it becomes the consuming passion of our life. Then comes the experience of God: intoxicated on the Spirit, ravished by the Bridegroom, delighted in by the Father—dancing with the Trinity. It's the source of our deepest joy, the real point of living.

If that's true, and I believe it is, then the greatest commitment I can make in my life is to discover my desire for God and indulge that passion with all my soul. And the greatest miracle that can happen is to have my passion stirred, ignited, and released until I actually feed on God.

You can do that for me. And I can do it for you. It doesn't

always require a scare like cancer or a tragic plane crash. We can bring that miracle into each other's lives. We can learn to talk with each other in ways that arouse our passion for God until it becomes the most powerful desire in our soul. How that can happen, and what needs to happen in you and me as we speak into each other's lives, is what this book is all about.

It's about learning a language that has the power to pull back the curtains on our soul, to move through the mess, and to help each other discover that what we really want is God. The language with the power to make that happen is what I call SoulTalk. It's the only really *honest* language.

THE POWER OF SOULTALK

Every day, all across the world, people talk to each other. Unless we're asleep or locked up in solitary confinement, we're talking to each other, all the time.

Now just imagine what could happen if Jesus followers in every country on earth learned to talk in a way that released supernatural power, a power that was literally the power of God. Suppose Christians all over the world learned to speak SoulTalk.

That's the vision behind this book: parents speaking SoulTalk whether their kids are sweet preschoolers or drug-abusing teenagers or divorcing adults; husbands and wives switching to SoulTalk in the middle of a fight and avoiding divorce or, worse, a dead marriage that continues; husbands speaking SoulTalk to wives when childhood abuse is remembered; wives speaking

SoulTalk to their husbands when a job is lost; friends in small groups or in one-on-one conversations speaking a language that carries them into God's presence; elder boards, business colleagues, golfing buddies, mission teams, church staffs, counselors and counselees—all speaking SoulTalk.

It can happen! God wants to see it happen. He's made every provision for it to happen. *This dream can come true.* It's God's plan!

But first, we'll need to understand the real battle going on in our soul, why we feel pressured so often and get so tired, why it's so hard to change even when we really want to. We'll need to admit how angry we sometimes feel, how distant we sometimes are from our mate, how we've put our children ahead of our partner and even ahead of God, and how reasonable and noble it feels to do so. We'll need to face how disconnected we truly are from others and how our church experience sometimes leaves us feeling even more isolated and alone.

Before discouragement defeats us, we'll need to know that God's Spirit is still at work, that he has the power to turn every obstacle to happiness into a doorway to God, and that he does his best work through Jesus followers who learn to speak SoulTalk. It's time for a revolution in relationships, for Christians across the world to release their passion for God and to ignite that passion in others, to speak with power into each other's lives.

But it will take some honest soul-searching. Too many of us think we're doing fine in our conversations when all we're speaking is SelfTalk.

Soul Talk

Meister Eckhart, a wise medieval spiritual director, once said, "God is at home; it is we who have gone out for a walk." We've all left home. We're not even looking for the face of God. Second things have become first in our affections. SelfTalk is the language we speak when we don't realize that what we really want is God. We speak it more fluently, more religiously, when we think we want God but in fact want only to use him to grant our wish list. SelfTalk, religious or secular, is the language of people who have left home and are trying to make a rented apartment feel like home.

It's time to return, to come home to our own soul, where God has chosen to live, and to speak from our soul to the souls of others. If we do, we will ignite a revolution.

People all across the world will trade in passing pleasures for lasting satisfaction. When troubles come—and they will—we'll not give up or settle for relief. We'll not cave in on ourselves even more, because we'll be living to know someone bigger, better, and more important than ourselves, someone who promised to hold us secure till the dark night ends and the bright morning comes. We'll cling to him, not to dreams of how our life should turn out.

We'll connect, and we'll draw close to a handful of friends as together we live to draw closer to God. And best of all, we'll actually strike up a friendship with each member of the Trinity. We'll feel like poorly dressed party crashers who are welcomed into the fanciest mansion we've ever seen, dressed instantly in the finest clothes perfectly fitted, and then invited to dance and dine with the three hosts for a very long time, beginning now.

That's what life is all about. I learned it in the hospital. I believe God kept me alive so I could speak about it, so together we could start dancing with God. Then we'll learn SoulTalk, and we'll speak with power into people's lives, especially the people we love the most.

1

THE SOULTALK REVOLUTION

Speaking Words of Life to Each Other

I T'S TRUE AT EVERY LEVEL OF SOCIETY, in every culture. Whether you're at the top of the money ladder, hovering near the bottom, or struggling to stay on a middle rung; whether you're a successful pastor instructing seminary students or an unheralded missionary barely surviving on dwindling support; whether you're a face-lifted, tummy-tucked socialite deciding which of your clubs to dine at tonight or a schoolteacher brown-bagging it in the cramped faculty lounge; it's all the same.

Most people go through their entire life never speaking words to another human being that come out of what is deepest within them, and most people never hear words that reach all the way into that deep place we call the soul.

Behind bedroom doors and boardroom doors, in church staff meetings and small groups, on golf carts breezing along to the next tee box and on church leadership retreats convened to discuss vision and budgets and facility needs, in cars carrying excited kids to Disney World and in planes carrying Christian conference junkies to the next big event, it's all the same. We chat, argue, plan, gossip, pray, flatter, lie, maneuver, preach, and tell stories no one listens to about old friends who retired or divorced or got sick. We say, "Wonderful to see you" to people we wish would go away; we discuss world problems, debate religious issues, despair over declining culture, debunk diet fads, divulge confidences that draw us artificially closer to our confidants, and distract ourselves with details about Tiger Woods's latest heroics on the golf course or Kevin Costner's latest box office flop. In therapists' offices or pastors' studies, sometimes on back decks while steaks sizzle on the grill, we quietly reveal sexual struggles, emotional struggles, job struggles, spiritual struggles, money struggles. And the same thing happens all the time.

We almost never speak words that are formed in the center of our soul and pour out from our very being with power and a sense of life.

We almost never speak words that are formed in the center of our soul and pour out from our very being with power and a sense of life. And we almost never hear words that stir life within us, that pour hope into those empty spaces deep inside filled only with fear and fury and frustration.

Over lunch, we listen to and share stories about ego-driven spiritual leaders who, out of the public eye, are control freaks and threatening tyrants; about Christian businesspeople who live for the next deal but never miss church; about the poor and disadvantaged whose plight we discuss to comfort ourselves with the illusion that talking about them proves our concern for them. We read about ghetto gangs and prostitutes and porn addicts and the older couple who committed suicide by jumping together from their eighteenth-floor window. We hear about neglected missionaries and disillusioned doctors and cynical church people and desperate singles and more desperate marrieds and distraught parents whose stories we pass on in order to come across as concerned and authentic.

We wag our heads with a *What's this world coming to?* attitude while we grab our next supersized combo at McDonald's or tell the wine steward to bring us another bottle of Cabernet. "Something simply must be done about all these problems," we tell each other. If our life is relatively comfortable, we do nothing, or at least nothing that disrupts our comfort. If we're less comfortable or more sensitive, we go on spiritual retreats, sign up for the latest Bible study program, start a prayer journal, or get more involved in church or community service. And as Christians, we relax a bit knowing some churches are doing things to make a difference in this sorry world. Megachurches have programs to reach every conceivable "need group." Influential and well-known Christians push their agendas with prophetic zeal and wear themselves out doing all that needs to be done to change the world.

Politicians peddle solutions for social problems, economic problems, and security problems that promise more than they ever deliver; nice people volunteer to drive the elderly to doctors' appointments and to mentor on-the-edge kids and to bring meals to shut-ins; college professors write books that shape thought in ivory towers; seminaries adapt their teaching models to fit a postmodern culture; and evangelists and conference leaders look for ways to get their message out. And all the while, it stays the same.

People across the world remain alone—personally unknown, personally unobserved, and personally untouched. We rarely speak words that connect who we are beneath our pretense, posturing, and political correctness to another living soul. *We rarely hear words that draw our soul into the soul of another human being and, together, into God.*

Churches, by no means all but too many, have become as dangerous to the health of our soul as porn shops. People leave both superficially titillated and deeply numbed. Religious events can be as irrelevant to real life as cocktail parties at country clubs: "Oh, you just redecorated your home? How wonderful. You must tell me all about it" or, "Wasn't that just a beautiful sermon? The illustrations, the stories—I felt so moved." Christian organizations dedicated to reaching people with the gospel struggle internally with moral compromise, relational division, and strutting egos. Christian crusaders push for biblical literacy and expository preaching and abortion protesting and porn shop closing, and their words seem energized more by power-hungry moralism and grace-lacking legalism than by engagement with culture on behalf of a holy *and loving* God. And without a noticeable shift in tone or mood, religious conversation turns to market woes and prudent investment strategies and fund-raising opportunities.

Retired folks in coffee shops gripe about expensive prescriptions or brag about their children's success or lament their infrequent visits. Middle-agers share stories about problem teens, pursue whatever dreams are left, and worry about growing old. Younger adults talk about babies, new jobs, exciting churches and ministries, and Grandpa's inheritance. Adolescents choose heroes, fit in or drop out, talk big or talk dirty, and carve out their unique identities as zealous Christians, free spirits, thoughtful introverts, sexy head-turners, or bold nonconformists. And preadolescents idolize Britney Spears and rap stars. Through it all, in every age group, in every social group, in every religious group, it's all the same.

Most people tuck their soul out of sight and try desperately to ignore that something is missing they can't supply. We speak few words that come out of an honest look into our soul, and few words are spoken to us that inspire the courage to take an honest look, that give us hope that painful authenticity could lead to real life. *Existential*

For most human beings across the world, life goes on. Every internal reality is felt—excitement, fear, pressure, anger, happiness, boredom, fulfillment, emptiness, misery, delight, anticipation, compassion, indifference, snobbishness, shame, religious awe—every internal reality except *life*. We cannot experience the love and joy of real life until we're connected to another at the level of our soul. We cannot know the freedom to be who we truly are until we yield who we really are to another and experience that person's acceptance. We cannot move into our world with other-centered energy and noble purpose as long as we remain alone—unknown, unexplored, undiscovered, and untouched. The life of God is not pouring out of us into others.

We rarely speak with power into a person's life. Or, if we do, it's divisive power, destructive power. But it could be different.

LEARNING TO SPEAK SOULTALK

It's time to put the center in the center. Coming together at the level of soul with the supernatural power supplied only by Jesus Christ must be the foundation of every other good thing we do. And it can happen. Not in big crowds, but in small pockets, two or three at a time, groups of eight or ten. We could discover the life that is already in us as Jesus followers, and we could speak that life into others and receive that life when it comes to us from another.

We cannot experience the love and joy of real life until we're connected to another at the level of our soul.

That's SoulTalk—speaking whatever is truly alive in us into another and accepting whatever is truly alive in another when it is spoken into us.

Be aware. SoulTalk is radically different from SelfTalk. SelfTalk is the natural language of every person ever born, except Jesus. It's the language of self-protection and self-sufficiency and self-absorption. It's the language of noble ambition and generous involvement and moral concern and life-improving agendas that tries to do high good without commitment to the highest good.

SelfTalk is our social language, our religious language, our political language, our business language, our relationship language. It comes from someplace other than our Spirit-saturated center. It comes out of our efforts to adjust to this world, to make it a better place, to get along comfortably in it, to keep ourselves happy and fulfilled and safe and to help others feel better about themselves and about their lives. It speaks death and smothers souls.

It's the language we all speak naturally and will continue to speak all the way to our grave—unless the Spirit of God intervenes and we respond.

The Spirit has intervened.

He is right now intervening.

It's time for us to respond.

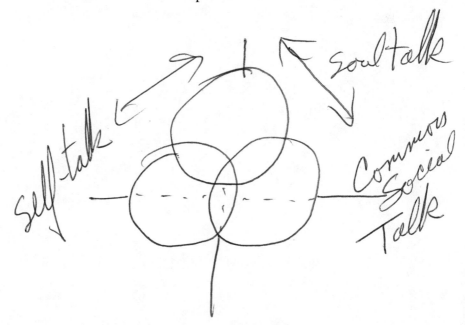

2

WE NEED A NEW WAY TO RELATE

The Old Way Isn't Working

I'M IN A FUNK. You know it as soon as we sit down for lunch. There's none of the usual, "Hey, old man, how ya doin'?" Instead, I greet you with a tight smile and a weak, "Hi."

You know something's wrong. Anyone could pick that up. But what should you do? You're a good friend. Maybe it's just another one of my bad moods. Perhaps you should wait it out. Keep things pleasant, and I'll get over it. I always do.

But more is going on in you. You vaguely notice a few feelings cropping up in you as you order your meal. Disappointment. Weariness. A hint of impatience, a *Here we go again* reaction to my low. Unbidden thoughts flow into your mind, thoughts you immediately realize you better not share with me. *I just found out my kid's sleeping with his girlfriend, and he's in a bad mood. His two sons are doing great, last I heard—happily married, walking with the Lord. What's he got to be down about? Well, probably something. We've all got problems. I was hoping to talk to him about my son, but maybe I'll wait. Looks like I need to be here for him today.*

So, with only a little reluctance, you give me center stage by asking, "Is everything OK? You seem down."

Something in me snaps. I feel instantly mad.

But why? You were asking about me, exactly what I wanted you to do. You picked up the cue and read the script. But the way you read it annoyed me. "Is everything OK?" *What a stupid question. Would I seem down if everything were OK? You don't really want to know. You want nothing to be all that wrong so you won't have too much to handle in dealing with me.* Sometimes I wonder if anyone would stay involved with me if they knew everything that was going on inside. Even I have to stay away from everything inside me or *I'd* go crazy.

Well, I'm being too hard on you, I think. You are a good friend. And you did ask how I was doing. I'll take a risk. I'll let you in on some of what's bothering me, then I'll see what you do with it.

I stir cream into my coffee, take a sip, and say a little off-handedly, "I'm just really tired. I've got a deadline to meet and I'm not making much progress. It's getting to me, I guess. But I've been here before. I'll be all right." *There! I opened the door. Do you want to hear more? Will you try to fix me? Or will you hear me?*

You feel genuine concern but not a lot of warmth—you're still thinking about your son, and that whole scene feels like a much bigger problem than mine—but you *are* concerned. Yet you feel an edge as you get ready to respond. *I don't write books, so I can't relate to deadline pressures like his. But I understand pressure. I feel it all the time, especially now at home. His pressure, though, at least some of it,*

seems like it's his own making. Why does he agree to deadlines he can't meet?
It's not like this is his first book. Well, he does take on a lot. Letters, people,
speaking—but he could say no. He says yes then feels like the weight of the
world is on his shoulders. But I can't tell him that. He doesn't take that kind
of feedback too well.

So you put those thoughts aside and say instead, "You look
really tired. You going to get a chance to rest at all? Maybe play
some golf?"

"Not for a while."

Now you're annoyed. You can feel it. The edge has matured
into outright irritability. You sense my pull: *Feel sorry for me, tell*
me how hard I work, affirm the value of what I do. I can read it on your
face. You just don't *look* very empathic.

But you do care. You like me. You think what I'm doing
does matter. And you want to help. So you try to say something
helpful. "Couldn't you plan a month off after you finish this
project? I mean, you make your own schedule. Maybe just a
week? You know, no appointments. No nothing. Sounds like
you need it."

I know you mean well, I really do, and I appreciate it. So why
do I feel like getting up and leaving? Why do I feel so missed?
Am I just a whining baby, demanding attention when I should
just grow up and get on with my responsibilities? But I want
you to listen. I want so badly to be seen and heard. Why can't
you ask more questions before you give me advice? Don't try
to solve my problem. That's not what I'm asking you to do. I
wish you wouldn't hear me share one problem, assume that's the
whole picture, and then try to fix it. Why can't you—someone,

anyone—stop trying to fix what you think is wrong, stop trying to make me feel better, and just hear me, be with me? I just want someone to know me and still want me. And you're not doing that!

But we're friends. I know I sometimes drive you crazy, and you've put up with my moods for a long time. I value our friendship, and I don't want to mess it up. So I say, "Yeah, I really would love a month off. Sounds great. But I don't see it happening. Probably not even a week. And I'm not even sure it's supposed to happen. I know I don't manage my life very well; I take on too much—but I remember something Francis Schaeffer said in one of his books. He said that modern Christians are so committed to their own personal peace and affluence that they never get to really know God. I agree with that. I see it in myself. Yes, I do like playing golf, and nothing's wrong with sitting by a pool with a good novel, and I do that sometimes. But I really do wonder if any of us has a clue about what it means to actually experience God and to enjoy him more than a great vacation."

Now you're feeling lectured to. You're not drawn to what I'm saying. I was thinking you should be taking notes; instead, you were waiting for your turn to speak. A wall's gone up. Now you don't *want* to listen. Before it didn't occur to you. But now you feel like arguing, addressing the jury on behalf of the defendant I'm prosecuting.

"Yeah, I agree with that. We're supposed to do whatever it takes to know God. But, man, people need to rest. Even Jesus got away, not to a resort, I grant you, but he spent whole nights with his Father. Taking some kind of break is good; it's necessary. It's part of what's required to know God. At least that's what I think. Maybe you ought to go on a spiritual retreat."

Whatever it was that snapped in me ten minutes ago just sagged. I feel tired as I hear your last comment, more resigned than defensive, more weary than mad. I desperately want to take a spiritual retreat somewhere in the mountains. A cabin, a rippling stream, tall pines, foxes, maybe a spiritual director for an hour a day, maybe no one. It sounds wonderful. I'm on the verge of tears.

I'm still feeling missed, more told what to do than heard and released. So I stiffen. I can feel it. I want to acknowledge your point, but I don't want to give in. And I *surely* don't want to collapse. I stand my ground, sort of. I smile tightly and say, "I had a guy write me awhile back and tell me in no uncertain terms I needed to get away with God for a while. He told me he was afraid I'd unravel if I didn't. And when I told my doctor how tired I was, she told me I was depressed and handed me a prescription for Zoloft. But I don't know. I see everything, even feeling down, as a doorway to knowing God better, not as a problem to be fixed with a spiritual retreat or a pill."

Again you feel . . .

And so it goes. Two good friends, having a conversation that frustrates us both—a conversation at two levels, one spoken and one unspoken. Unspoken were all the thoughts and feelings inside us that we dared not say. Spoken were the words that we hoped would make our point and keep the conversation—and our friendship—going.

Brothers in Christ, sincere followers of Jesus,

Every conversation either stimulates or dampens our desire for God.

and we walked away from an hour and a half of talking, feeling weary, uninvigorated, and less excited about the gospel than when our conversation began. No life-giving connection. No passion for God ignited. No deepened inclination to worship. Every conversation either stimulates or dampens our desire for God. This one was dampening. No SoulTalk, and therefore no power.

Instead, we engaged in ninety minutes of SelfTalk—an opportunity missed, squandered, wasted. Two souls could have met, but they didn't. Why? What went wrong?

A few hours before he died, Jesus asked his Father to make the people who would follow him "as unified and together as we are. . . . Then they'll be mature in this oneness, and give the godless world evidence that you've sent me" (John 17:22–23).

Why were two followers of Jesus two thousand years later more separated than united by our time together? Why would a video of our conversation incite no one to want Jesus?

Let me rephrase the question this way. It's the question I wrote this book to answer: *How can conversations between followers of Jesus become a stage on which the supernatural power of God is unmistakably displayed, where souls come alive, where life is enjoyed, where love is released and souls connect?*

THE DESTRUCTIVENESS OF SELFTALK

What went wrong in our lunch conversation? Why was Jesus' prayer for us not answered as we talked? Consider this.

We hid from each other what felt most real in us because we thought that sharing it would have harmed our relationship. Authenticity, when all that we can see to "authentically" share with another is natural rather than supernatural, severely damages relationships. Souls are hurt when people are authentically natural. *— only half-honesty*

It's all SelfTalk, authentic SelfTalk with destructive power.

- We were each *aware* of only natural thoughts and feelings in our soul, so in the name of friendship, we put a positive spin on what was going on inside, and out came another variety of SelfTalk. Call it socialized SelfTalk. We did our best to spiritualize and Christianize what was natural within us, and all we could offer each other was cleaned-up pettiness, friendly self-centeredness, socialized SelfTalk with no power. *Better to call it natural — only talk vs self — talk*

- What we failed to see was the divine life that was buried deep in our soul, throbbing at the exact center of our being, that could have been authentically released with no spin and would have aroused our desire to know God. Had each of us become aware of the thoughts and feelings stirred by God's Spirit in our spirit, and had we let those thoughts and feelings express themselves in words, we would have spoken SoulTalk; we would have spoken with power, good power, into each other's life. *✳*

Revelatory Talk ≈ prophetic talk

But we didn't see the miracle of new life within us. Awareness of our irritability and demands and insecurities crowded out any possible recognition of what was most alive and good and powerful within us. So we had to wear masks, like actors in a Greek tragedy, for the sake of keeping our relationship pleasant. And it's a good thing we did.

Imagine my friend saying to me, "Your lectures are boring" or me saying to my friend, "I thought your question was really stupid." Our friendship would have been dealt a severe, possibly lethal blow. Without seeing Christ's life within us, our choices are either authentic SelfTalk (say what you really feel and risk destroying relationships and harming souls) or socialized SelfTalk (spin what you feel into courteous conversation and preserve shallow relationships that keep everyone's soul pleasant and empty).

Jesus gives us a third option. Through the gospel, we have become participants in the divine nature; the life of God is now in us, located at the center of our soul. That life is both *propositional* and *passionate*. It has content and energy. It is true and alive. In all Jesus followers, there is a power inside that if identified, stirred up, and authentically released, will generate SoulTalk. We will speak words of life, water for thirsty souls, sentences that will energize people when they're weary and make the temptation to find enjoyment in counterfeit life less appealing.

HOW TO SPEAK SOULTALK

So how do we do it? What would it look like if we dug deep and became aware of the river of life flowing through our soul that is pressing for release in the words we speak to others? What would it take to speak with power into each other's life? That brings us back to our key question: *How can conversations between followers of Jesus become a stage on which the supernatural power of God is unmistakably displayed?*

I want to ask you to sit with me, just the two of us, and let me tell you my understanding of SoulTalk, what it is and how we can speak it. It will take some time. We'll need to get together more than once. Think of each chapter in this book as a separate conversation in which I share one more lesson in learning SoulTalk. No one dances the foxtrot right away. We learn one movement at a time and then keep at it until each movement flows together in graceful rhythm.

In SoulTalk, each movement we'll learn is another way to look into the interior world of the soul, into your soul and mine and into the souls of all the people we love.

Keep in mind that SoulTalk is the language of SoulCare. I don't want to confuse you with terms. Think of SoulCare as a special kind of relationship, an encounter with a supernatural *purpose.* The agenda, as we tag along behind the Spirit, is to see someone's appetite for God become the ruling passion of his or her life. If you are "in the pains of childbirth until Christ is formed" in someone's soul (Galatians 4:19 NIV), you are in a relationship of SoulCare.

SoulTalk is the language we speak in that relationship. It is language with supernatural passion and wisdom in the service of a supernatural purpose. We are speaking SoulTalk when the words we utter are formed by the passion to see another person want God more than anything else and by the wisdom of the

Spirit, who knows how to make that happen. SoulTalk then is carried out of our mouth in specific sentences by that same passion and wisdom, with only the prayer that the Spirit will use our words for his purposes. There's no power struggle in SoulTalk.

At this point, it may all sound too complicated, out of your reach. You're just an ordinary follower of Jesus, a normal person who's trying to live your life well, pay your bills, and be good to people—no special gifts, no mystical experiences, no advanced training in anything "deep."

But listen! You're not just an "ordinary" person. As C. S. Lewis said, no one is "a mere mortal."[1] If you're a Jesus follower, your soul is alive with God. The actual life of the Trinity is in this moment flowing through you. You are hungry for God, hungrier for him than for anything else.

And that life, that hunger, can come out of you through your words, your tone of voice, your uncontrived facial expressions. SoulTalk is not a high-level skill that only graduate students in spirituality can learn. It's a passion and an energy that's already in you, waiting to be released.

It's not a foreign language. It's the language you were born to speak. It's the language of the Spirit, who took up residence in your soul when you were born again into God's family. *Now you can speak like he does!*

THE FIVE STAGES OF SOULCARE

Let me anticipate what we'll discuss as we meet together through this book. SoulCare is a relationship that cycles through five stages. The more clearly you understand each stage, the more fluently you'll speak SoulTalk. The five stages are these:

First, *think beneath.* See the real battle that's being fought in someone's soul. It will require supernatural discernment to think beneath the problems people share and identify the battle going on in their soul that most folks never see.

Second, *think vision.* Capture the real plan of the Spirit—why he enters people's soul and what he is up to. It will require supernatural imagination to capture a vision of what the Spirit longs to do in someone's life. You'll know you're getting a clear picture when you feel thoroughly inadequate to make the Spirit's plan happen and when you can sense God's excitement as he anticipates it happening.

Third, *think passion.* Face the real mess that exists in your own soul as you speak with someone else. It will require supernatural courage to admit how subtly concern for your own ego disguises itself as real love. But you must see your own mess clearly before you'll be able to see the mess in another person's soul with clarity and without judgment. *≈ Narrative Tx*

Fourth, *think story.* Meet the real person you are talking with. Be curious about the story he is reluctant to tell and about the *The Lie* shaping events of his life, through which he learned what to value more than God. It will require supernatural listening to become a safe enough person that another will want to be explored by you.

Fifth, *think movement.* Follow the Spirit as he penetrates every defense against brokenness and every layer of self-sufficiency until the true self that he has created is released to love God as the supreme treasure of the human soul and to love others on behalf of Christ, at any cost. It will require supernatural rhythm to keep in step with God's Spirit as he dances into someone's soul.

BEFORE YOU BEGIN

One last thought as we begin our journey of discovering and practicing SoulTalk.

- If you feel overwhelmed, that's good. Only people overwhelmed by their inadequacy learn to listen to the Spirit as he teaches us to speak his language, SoulTalk.

- If you feel skeptical, wondering if the following chapters are merely pop psychology in religious dress, stick with me. I think you'll see that SoulTalk is not simplistically shallow or predictably formulaic. It can be spoken by the most advanced psychotherapist and the most mystical spiritual director, as well as by counselors, pastors, and friends. It's a language fully available and well suited to "ordinary" people who want to speak with power into other people's lives.

- If you feel stirred, then sign up with the Spirit as a revolutionary. He's the general. You're joining an army of people who are called to give evidence, by speaking SoulTalk, that Jesus is the only Lover and Satisfier of the human soul. Ask God to start a revolution in relationships, one relationship at a time, starting with *your* relationships. Pray that the revolution will spread until people across the world are given the chance to be safely known, graciously explored, hopefully discovered, and powerfully touched.

Now let's begin learning SoulTalk!

3

PAY CLOSE ATTENTION TO WHAT'S INSIDE

Beginning to Learn the Language of SoulTalk

I HAVE JUST ONE REQUEST AS WE GET GOING," I told our instructor, Heather, when my wife and I met her for our first dance lesson. "Make sure you start at the beginning! Assume I know nothing and you won't be far off."

She smiled warmly—a little too quickly, I thought—and then said, "No problem. We'll take it slow and easy. You guys will do just fine, I can tell. Now, where shall we start? Do you want to learn swing, the Viennese waltz, the foxtrot, cha-cha? What did you have in mind?"

Heather wasn't getting the picture.

"I want to move my feet without stepping on hers. I don't want to trip over my own, and I don't want to make a total fool of myself. And I want to have fun. *That's* what I have in mind."

Her vision cleared. I could tell by her fading smile. More thoughtful and appropriately subdued, she said, "So what you do now on the dance floor is the sway. You pretty much stand still and move your upper body back and forth a little."

Heather got the picture. We started from the beginning.

That's where I want us to begin as we learn the language of SoulTalk. Let's start at the beginning.

THE BEGINNING OF SOULTALK

The beginning is where you are. What do you feel, what are you thinking, when people share something with you? Maybe it's a secret, maybe a struggle they've told no one else—and now they're telling you. What happens inside you as you listen?

What happens in me is still a surprise. I always feel inadequate. *Why are they telling me? What can I do? Could words that I speak have any power?*

Sometimes I cover those painful feelings (as much to hide them from myself as from the person I'm talking with) with a false confidence, behind a silence that I try to convince myself is an opportunity for quiet thought. But inside I'm scrambling.

I feel clumsy, awkward, not prepared to speak with power into people's lives. I can't do it. I may be able to sound thoughtful, come across as caring, and offer a few reasonably perceptive comments—but can I speak with power? Will anything eternally important happen because words come out of my mouth? God spoke and the world appeared. Jesus spoke and Lazarus came alive. I speak and people yawn.

That may be where you are as you step onto the dance floor to talk to people. Or maybe not. If you feel rather polished and skillful and see yourself as bright enough and experienced enough to make a difference in people's lives, you may be aiming too low; or perhaps you've done a better job than I have of covering your insecurity. I used to do a better job than I do now.

To my shame, I remember telling a class of counseling students years ago that if anyone would hang in there long enough with me I could help that person. I could *always*, given enough time, help *anyone* who came to see me. I must have taken a pride pill that morning, laced with a pretty strong dose of denial.

If you are willing to live with an honest awareness of inadequacy, if you are willing to struggle with a host of strange and difficult feelings as you speak with people, then you are ready to learn SoulTalk.

OVERCOMING FEELINGS OF INADEQUACY

There are only three ways to escape the painful experience of feeling inadequate in conversation.

First, *stick with a task you can handle,* such as social chitchat, instructing employees on their responsibilities, discussing plans with colleagues, making your point in an argument, teaching a class, preaching a sermon, selling a product, telling jokes, being honest with your spouse, confiding in friends, or listening to friends when they confide in you.

Second, *aim low.* Ease tension, smooth over conflict, convince someone of something, encourage someone to keep on, help a friend feel better, build a religious organization and call it a church, relieve symptoms of emotional distress with distraction or medication or professional therapy, make a younger child conform to your expectations, keep a marriage functioning, or end a friendship in the name of tough love.

Third, *live in denial.* Pretend your training, talents, godliness, maturity, experience, verbal agility, quick mind, warm demeanor, wide reading background, reputation, degrees, Bible knowledge, creative understanding of psychological theory— pretend that *something* about you gives you the power to speak deeply into another person's soul and to arouse a deep, exhilarating sense of being wonderfully alive.

But if you *don't* stick with a task you are competent to handle but rather enter the battle for someone's soul, if you *don't* aim low but rather long to see someone actually want God more than any other thing in life, and if you *don't* live in denial but rather confess that you have exactly no power to do anything of eternal consequence in anyone's life, then you're walking onto the dance floor with the humility to learn—and to become a very good dancer.

THE RHYTHM OF THE SPIRIT

Let me tell you what Heather told me: "If I simply turn on the music and ask you to dance, you'll sway. But there's something already in you that maybe I can call forth and help release. It's *rhythm.* And if it's already there as much as I think it is, you will do just fine. You'll be dancing in no time. And you'll spend the rest of your life learning to dance even better."

Fellow Christian, follower of Jesus, the rhythm of the Spirit is already in you. There is a graceful power in each of us that will only flow out of a humble heart, but it *will* flow! It's one of those strange but true paradoxes: When you know you can't do it, you can. Only people who know they are blind ask for the power to see. Let's *think beneath* to see that power.

Nothing is more difficult for us "swayers" to believe than that everything we need to dance is already in us. And you will not discover the ordinary-looking power within you that is divinely extraordinary until you get into the real battle and see what is going on beneath the surface of people's lives, until you desperately want to see people change so deeply that they actually look a little more like Jesus, and until you call out to God with tears for power to be released from your soul that you had nothing to do with putting there.

Whatever I can do without the Spirit is SelfTalk; whatever I can do only with the Spirit is SoulTalk.

Here's the principle that will get us off to a good start: *Whatever I can do without the Spirit is SelfTalk; whatever I can do only with the Spirit is SoulTalk.*

It's taken me a long time to learn that principle. After more than thirty years as a clinical psychologist, counseling professor, and Bible teacher, I can empathize, probe, and interpret with the best of them (well, almost); and I know enough Bible to usually recognize which biblical principle applies to your particular struggle and to suggest a course of action.

I'm a pretty good listener. I ask a lot of questions, some that reach deep and provoke good thought. I really do care that things go better for people. I want your kids to do well, I want your marriage to be close, and I want your depression to lift. I generally communicate my concern with sensitivity and focused attention on your difficulties. And I've learned enough about grace to not be too judgmental.

After fifty years of following Jesus and thirty years of intense conversations about every imaginable struggle, I've got enough experience to address most of what I hear with pretty decent insight. I can see a fog-lifting perspective on a great variety of problems, and I can steer people in directions that are healthy and helpful.

And I can do all of that without the Spirit's power. My training, my talents, and my mind are quite sufficient. The one thing I can't do without the Spirit is speak with power into another person's soul. I can't discover and release divine energy within me or discern and communicate divine wisdom to another without the Spirit. If I am to speak divine passion and wisdom into another person's soul and arouse that person's desire for God, I must discern the Spirit's rhythm and yield to his purpose and pace.

I can speak into people's lives with psychological insight, human presence, relational skill, and moral clarity. But without sensing deep conviction that what I'm thinking is actually and directly from God, I have no power to change anyone's life as our lives are meant to be changed. Everything I say is SelfTalk.

SoulTalk, speaking with a power that can change lives, is altogether different. After all these years, I'm beginning to see the difference. And it's revolutionizing the way I relate.

I'm still learning the basics of SoulTalk. But the prospect of relating to God in a way that settles every question about who I am and what life is all about, the anticipation of knowing God in a way that frees me to enter your life not to settle my questions, but to speak to yours, has captured me. It could change the way we practice counseling, the way we do church, the way we relate to our spouse and parent our kids, the way we structure our small group meetings, the way we carry on business and set goals, and the way we build friendships.

For me, it's the New Way to live and to relate. Paul described it as "the new way of the Spirit" and contrasted it with "the old way of the written code" (Romans 7:6 NIV). No longer do I need to try to do everything right when I'm talking with you—the pressure's off.

Now I can enter into a dance with you in which sometimes we move quickly, sometimes slowly. Sometimes we're so close we touch; other times we back away to permit each of us to move in our own way. It's a new way to relate, and it depends entirely on feeling the rhythm of the Spirit in us, trusting that rhythm and abandoning ourselves to it, following his call to movement.

This New Way of relating, of speaking with power into people's lives because we've been spoken to by God with his power, is a fire in my bones, and I can't hold it in. So let's start dancing.

THINK BENEATH

Here's how I suggest you begin to speak SoulTalk. When someone shares a struggle, resist the urge to run, resist the urge to help, and resist the urge to refer. Instead, *think beneath*. Let me explain the difference.

Suppose your husband drags himself in the door at 7:30 P.M., plops wearily on the sofa, and says, "This was the kind of day where I just wish someone would shoot me."

Think beneath to what is most alive in you and to what is most conflicted in him.

Listen before you speak. You've heard his words, but you may not have heard his soul.

Resist the urge to run! Don't retreat in terror ("Omigosh! He's suicidal!") or disgust ("Nice to have him care how *my* day went").

Resist the urge to help! Don't let your panic or your compassion drive you to think about how you could cheer him up or lighten his load. That could be tough. People "pull" us to help, to do something they will find valuable. We want to help our friends and loved ones, though not always for noble reasons. You may feel a compulsion to do or say something your husband will thank you for. Resist that compulsion.

Resist the urge to refer! Don't assume, even though past experience may make it hard not to, that nothing you can say or do will reach him. Don't say that he's determined to be a grump or he's struggling with clinical depression or he's not really interested in anything you can offer, so you might as well suggest he call a friend or talk to the pastor or see a therapist.

Put your mind to work. It will require discipline on your part. It will be a choice. But if you do it often enough, it will feel like taking a first step in rhythm with dance music. The choice you make is this: *Think beneath* to what is most alive in you and to what is most conflicted in him. What stirs most deeply in you, and what is the real battle he is fighting? *Think beneath.* Reflect on what is happening beneath the surface of your interaction until you discover the life in you and the battle in him.

Let me spend the rest of this chapter *thinking beneath* about the life that is in every follower of Jesus.

THE LIFE OF GOD IN US

We live in a day when the life that God has given to every Jesus follower is counterfeited, contrived, neglected, hidden, un-released, and generally not believed in. If we're going to discover the life within us that will enable us to speak with power into people's lives, we'll have to give up hope of speaking with obvious miraculous power. Making someone fall down on a stage in front of thousands of people and claiming that person was slain in the Spirit requires showmanship, a herd mentality where the expectation of many people has the power to influence behavior, and the desperation of lost hope.

As Jesus' ministry continued, his obvious miracles became fewer, and quiet miracles took their place. The miracle of his looking at three close friends who fell asleep when he needed them most and not getting mad, but walking away to die for them is far more impressive even than his raising the dead. One *impresses* us. The other *invites* us. It draws us to the hope of becoming that kind of person.

The SoulTalk I'm interested in has little to do with shouting "Be healed!" and everything to do with relating with the supernatural power of divine character, with loving people the way the Father and the Son love each other and the way Jesus, on behalf of the Father and in dependence on the Spirit, loves us. *That's* where the power is. *That's* the miracle we're after.

Martin Luther called it "left-handed" power. Right-handed power consists of the blatant demonstration of power *over* people. Left-handed power is the quiet demonstration of power *in* people, the power to stir up an appetite for God no matter what may be happening in someone's life. SoulTalk is about left-handed power. We'll see God's right-handed power when he returns to earth. For now, we can speak into people's lives with a power that can change them from the inside out.

THE GOSPEL'S POWER IN US

Begin your entry into the interior world of the human soul by focusing your thoughts on what is now in you because of the gospel. What energy is throbbing at the center of your being? What motivates you more than anything else? What do you most want to do, right now, as you interact with this person?

Read through a sample of biblical passages that can guide

your efforts to *think beneath.* Each one is taken from the contemporary language of *The Message,* Eugene Peterson's excellent effort to translate God's Word into the language of our day, the way it might sound if it were written to our culture.

> You don't need a telescope, a microscope, or a horoscope to realize the fullness of Christ. . . . When you come to him, that fullness comes together for you, too. His power extends over everything. (Colossians 2:9–10)

> Entering into this fullness is not something you figure out or achieve. . . . No, you're already in. . . . God brought you alive— right along with Christ. (Colossians 2:11, 13)

> People who try to run your life are "completely out of touch with the source of life, Christ . . . whose very breath and blood flow through you." (Colossians 2:18–19)

> The mystery in a nutshell is just this: Christ is in you . . . it's that simple. (Colossians 1:28)

> We've been given a brand-new life. . . . Your life is a journey you must travel with a deep consciousness of God. (1 Peter 1:3, 17)

> We were also given absolutely terrific promises to pass on to you—your tickets to participation in the life of God. (2 Peter 1:4)

I wake up every morning more aware of bad breath and lingering fatigue than supernatural power. Too much evidence, in how people respond to me and in how I feel and how I handle people, supports the notion that God's life is not in me. Or if it is, it's not yet ripe enough to enjoy.

If you are a follower of Jesus, then the energy and passion with which the members of the Trinity relate to each other is right now in you.

My father once told me how grateful he was for the opportunity to believe God's Word when nothing he felt or saw helped him to believe. He had just gone through a ten-day ordeal in the hospital following open-heart surgery.

On the way home from the hospital, he said to me, "So many good friends came to visit me during those awful days. But God never showed up. The One I wanted most to come never did. I never felt his presence for even a moment as I lay there in the hospital bed."

And then I heard his voice choke: "To think he trusted me to believe he was there just because he said he was, with no other evidence—I'm so grateful!"

Read the verses again. God is telling us something that rarely feels true. And it's this: *If you are a follower of Jesus, then the energy and passion with which the members of the Trinity relate to each other is right now in you.* The unconditional love of the Father, the indescribable grace of the Son, and the infinite patience of the Spirit are all, at this precise moment, alive in the center of your soul.

I know it doesn't always *feel* true. We're more aware of self-protective energy and self-serving passion and conditional love and frowning disapproval and irritable impatience. Those are all there, too, but they're not at the center of our soul. They don't define who we are. Christ defines who we are. The whole purpose of Christianity is to make us "little Christs." And the job is already under way. The Spirit of Christ—his passion and his wisdom—is already in us.

Think of the energy behind all that Jesus did, the passion that prompted every word he spoke. Jesus felt thirst—he asked for water. Jesus felt tired—he said no to some people and got away by himself. Jesus felt angry—he closed a few greed-based businesses. Jesus felt lonely—he asked a few special friends to be with him when he was hurting.

But beneath every secondary motive was a primary motive: *He loved God, and he loved to please him.* Nothing he ever wanted or felt or did compromised the passion that ruled in his soul. He loved God with all his being. His idea of deep pleasure, of "soul joy," had nothing whatsoever to do with prestige or recognition or accomplishments or success or approval from others or even intimacy with friends. He found his deepest satisfaction in God. His identity was centered in his Father.

Jesus was therefore able to give himself to others without demanding anything in return, to care with genuine other-centered passion, and to speak what was true without feeling threatened by the possibility of a negative response. With the passion to love God came the wisdom to reveal God. And it is that same passion and wisdom that is now in us!

AN EXAMPLE OF SOULTALK

When we speak from that life, we speak SoulTalk. A story will illustrate the point.

A pastor told me, "It feels like our church is hanging by a single thread. I can see the scissors ready to cut it and let our church collapse. There's a lot of division right now."

One longtime member, a close friend of the pastor, got his feelings hurt by something that took place in a committee meeting and threatened to leave. The pastor told me what happened.

"I met this guy for lunch. I felt like telling him to grow up. He seemed like a whining baby. I've had my feelings hurt a lot worse than his, and I'm sticking it out. I figured he should be able to do it too. And I was scared. I didn't want to lose him as a friend or from our church. But all those feelings seemed to come out of parts of me that felt really unclean. It was all about me and what I wanted.

"I remember looking at him across the table and thinking, *The real tragedy here is that he's cheating God out of the pleasure of having his heart, and he's cheating himself of joy in the process. He must be miserable to live with.* I really felt for his wife and kids.

"As I was thinking all this, I felt a quiet peace. Even if the church folds, I'll be all right. Yeah, sometimes I wake up at two in the morning in a panic worried about it, and I can feel really ticked at this guy for wanting to leave. But none of that's deepest in me. I really want to be close to God more than I want our church to flourish. So I didn't feel like I needed my friend to do anything, not to be my friend, not to stay with the church, not even to pursue God. But I wanted all those things, mostly the last. So I just told him that."

Whatever comes out of our mouth when our heart is ruled by our passion for God is SoulTalk. Whatever we say to another when we're emptied enough of our natural passions to be filled with the life of Jesus has supernatural power. It may not be obvious. Nothing might happen that we can see. But the Spirit is doing his work.

That's the beginning. We have the life of God in us, and that life can arouse in another person the desire for God.

But that's just the beginning. We're still swaying, but we're about to start dancing.

Next up: *Think beneath* to the battle.

ask yourself / ask the Spirit —
what do you want me to say to
him / her?.

4

WANT GOD MORE THAN ANYTHING ELSE

Seeing the Real Battle in a Person's Soul

WE'RE FIGHTING THE WRONG BATTLE. We're excited about things that bore God, things that stir us up then tire us out. Another initiative. Another campaign. Another way to do it. We're putting our energy and resources into projects and programs that market well but don't do what God most wants done.

Which is worse? A church program to build community that doesn't get off the ground or one person sitting every Sunday in the back of the church who remains unknown? A Sunday school class that once drew hundreds but has now dwindled to thirty or a Sunday school teacher whose sense of failure is never explored by a caring friend? A family torn apart by the father's drinking, his wife's frustration, and their third grader's learning disabilities or a self-hating dad, a terrified mom, and a lonely little boy, three human beings whose beauty and value no one ever discovers? A national campaign that fails to gain steam for the pro-life movement or a single woman on her way home from an abortion clinic in the backseat of a taxi, a woman whose soul no one ever touches?

We may notice the unknown pew sitter, we wonder how the teacher of the now-small class feels, we worry over each member of the torn-up family, and we feel for the guilt and pain of a woman who has ended her baby's life. But we do what's easier. We design programs, we brainstorm ways to build attendance, and in our outrage over divorce statistics and abortion numbers we fight for family values.

These are all good things, but we don't *talk* to the pew sitter; we don't *ask* the teacher how he's feeling; we don't *invite* the dad to play golf, the woman to lunch, or the little boy to play with our children; we don't let the aborting woman know we *care* about her soul. Time is one problem. But feeling uncomfortable in how we speak to struggling people is a bigger one. As a result, souls are never entered; people remain unknown, undiscovered, and untouched while programs flourish, ministries grow, and moral campaigns get press.

Programs, bigness, and moral indignation have become substitutes for SoulTalk. Many of us, of course, are disorganized, small, and indifferent to any kind of evil that doesn't touch our life directly. We stay to ourselves, committed to personal comfort, struggling along to make it happen. But as a culture, we depend on managed care for body and soul, we measure success by size, and we mistake outrage over sin for personal holiness and outrage over another's stupidity for personal wisdom. We're busy, big, and passionate, involved in everything but the real battle going on in the human soul. All across the world, people in record numbers are living the tragedy of an unobserved life. For people desperate to be noticed, forgiven, and wanted, there is no greater tragedy.

Spiritual America is leading the way. Visionaries call us to religious action. Entrepreneurs figure out how to get the action going. Marketing geniuses brand the action till everybody's talking about it. Gifted performers speak or sing us into action. Again, all good things with an important place—but not first place. More important is that each leader be known by someone, not by a crowd or a committee, but by a person, a close friend, an intimate companion. And not merely held accountable, but genuinely known in an intimate, vulnerable, painfully real, long-term relationship.

OUR DESIRE TO BE KNOWN

We know each other's names. We know what we do. We work together and discuss exciting things. We pray together. We enjoy each other and laugh together. But we remain personally unknown. No one knows the battle going on deep in our soul. We may not see it ourselves.

But it isn't a big deal. Why? Because we're all doing our job and we're all doing just fine. But are we?

"My people are broken—shattered!—and they put on band-aids, saying, 'It's not so bad. You'll be just fine.' But things are not 'just fine'!" (Jeremiah 6:14). So said God when he looked down on his people in Jeremiah's day.

"Wait a minute," we say. "We're really not shattered. Sure,

we're tired, we're working too hard, and there's occasional tension in our relationships. OK, we do feel lonely at times. But we're around people every day. We're too busy even to think about how we feel. And we're not going to get caught up in all that psychological navel-gazing and all that touchy-feely relational stuff. There's too much to do. If people would just be responsible and get busy, they wouldn't worry so much about their insides.

"Of course sex is a problem," we say. "Isn't it for everybody? But I'm not cheating on my mate. I don't turn on bad stuff in my hotel room late at night. I begin most every day with a quiet time, and I'm really pretty involved in our church. C'mon—I'm really doing just fine. I'm getting a lot of things done I never would if I took the time to really get to know people. I have plenty of friends."

I have walked off platforms after addressing crowds of fifty, five hundred, five thousand, and even fifty thousand. The first minute is the toughest. You know you weren't on, yet people say nice things; others look away. Or you know you were on, and everyone can't wait to shake your hand, to embrace you. Deep inside, either way, you feel alone. What you did matters more than who you are.

Something dies inside. No one wants to know you, no one seems interested in asking questions about what's happening in you, no one's excited to discover the life of God in you, and no one knows how to touch that life in you with the life in him or her. You want to quit. What's deepest in you doesn't matter to anyone else.

Peter Kreeft quotes an ex-professing Christian who became a Zen Buddhist: "I could find books and teachers who told me what the [Christian] doctrine was, but I could not find anyone who experienced the doctrine." Kreeft comments, "He didn't find experience among Christians. When he found it among Buddhists, he became one."[1]

My story is different. I can find many Christians, leaders and followers, who feel excited about their faith. I can find just as many who don't. But the cornerstone doctrine of the Christian faith is the Trinity. And I don't often experience what the three of them enjoy among each other in my relationships with Christians, even though that's the whole point of Christianity.

Few people puzzle me with how radically dependent they are on God and how deeply satisfied they are with just him.

Few people puzzle me with how radically dependent they are on God and how deeply satisfied they are with just him. I can explain most of the "joy" I see on the basis of blessings not everyone shares. But people with blessing-dependent joy have no power to speak into the souls of those who have not been similarly blessed.

I wonder if I puzzle anybody. At times the whole "Christian thing" feels like a sham, like a bunch of contrived, inauthentic busyness that never touches my soul and never releases me to touch somebody else's soul. If I didn't believe the Bible, I would have quit long ago.

I often sit with others in the crowd. Sincere, hungry people, each with a story to tell that no one has heard, who feel excited when the celebrity appears onstage. The message is dynamic, the music inspiring. They write checks to keep the ministry going. They hear reports of wonderful things happening, and they hear of the terrible problems yet to be addressed. They write more checks to help our leaders stamp out evil. They try hard to not let the word they hear return void by clamping on to whatever is practical and resolving to apply it to their lives. They eagerly read the latest Christian bestseller and join a book club to discuss it. And they get in another small group for fellowship, prayer, and Bible study. Again, all good things.

But most of us are never known by a safe friend, never explored by a curious friend, and never discovered by a hopeful friend. And that is a tragedy, as harmful to the soul as AIDS is to the body. Hearts are not changed. Or hearts that have been changed by the Spirit at conversion to Christ are not released. Why? We're not fighting the real battle going on in the human soul. We don't see it, so we don't fight it.

Consider three stories I recently heard directly from the folks involved.

A missionary doesn't fit in with the mission board's understanding of how he should behave. He's made some mistakes. The board offers to help him become the servant he should be. The missionary isn't sure whom to resent more: the board that has not taken the time to hear his heart or himself for not being worthy of their confidence. But bitterness is wrong. So he puts it aside and does what he can to fit in for the sake of the kingdom. No one sees the battle in his soul. The missionary doesn't see it himself.

A senior pastor agonizes over a youth leader who is long on energy and short on wisdom. Several parents and a few kids have written letters of complaint to the elders. Over a ten-month period, the pastor meets with the youth leader for breakfast, on the golf course, in both their homes for dinner, wanting to know him, to express his support, to raise difficult matters with the goal of releasing the youth leader's good heart. But the youth leader feels picked on, unfairly judged, unkindly criticized. He begins bad-mouthing the pastor to key parents who like what the youth leader has done for their kids. The pastor's integrity is questioned. The church threatens to split. The pastor wonders if he can go on. A few close friends feel his pain and stand by him, but no one sees his real battle.

Sincere, godly parents with a drug-using son attend a family conference. They hear a Christian leader tell how he and his wife guided their four children into spiritual maturity, trusting God all the way. He finishes his presentation by inviting each of his children, all now young adults, to share their testimony for the glory of God. The last word belongs to the father: "Remember! God is faithful. He keeps his promise. If we raise our kids by his principles, they will become the joy of our heart." While the audience erupts into stand-up applause, the two parents quietly leave, feeling like total failures, discouraged and alone, wondering what they did wrong. They continue to pray for their son and to do all they can to get him off drugs.

But they never fight—or even see—the real battle going on in their own souls.

Brothers and sisters, *we are fighting the wrong battle!* The real battle for people's souls has yet to be engaged.

THE REAL BATTLE IN OUR SOUL

Only the Father loves us as we long to be loved. Only Jesus can change our heart. Only the Spirit can fill our soul with joy and peace and love. We know that. But what we don't know is that not until we speak with power into each other's life will people feel that love, experience that change, and release that life that is now in the soul of every Jesus follower and could be in everyone's soul. We'll enter the battle with power when we learn to speak SoulTalk, and then people will want God more than anything else.

But we're busy with other things. We're trying to make something happen or to join the folks who are already making things happen. We're trying to fit in with our leaders so we can be on the team, to manage our staff according to proven principles of leadership and conflict management so our organization runs smoothly, to parent our kids so one day they can be exhibited for the glory of God.

We're trying hard to be more spiritual, to trust God more, to deal with our problems, to stop complaining so much, to feel more passionate about the important things people are doing, to feel less depressed, to juggle all our responsibilities, to keep everyone happy, to like church more, to be more positive, to feel less guilty and less pressured, and to relate better to our mates, our kids, and our friends.

Jesus looks out across modern culture, over the crowds gathered in places of worship, in big arenas, at conference centers, into the faces of people meeting around board tables, in living rooms, at coffee shops. And with a breaking heart filled with hope, he says, "Are you tired? Worn out? Burned out on religion? Come to me. Get away with me and you'll recover your life" (Matthew 11:28–29).

And then he asks us to pray, to plead with God that he would raise up men and women who would care for souls, authentic people who would speak deeply into others' lives. Two thousand years ago, he said the world was ready for SoulTalk. It was ready then. It's ready now, perhaps more than ever.

Years earlier, back in Old Testament times, God had been watching his people gather for worship, and he saw how determined they were to make their lives work. No one was enjoying him. They were too busy trying to "live religiously" so that their lives would go well. In exasperation, he cried out, "Why doesn't one of you just shut the Temple doors and lock them? Then none of you can get in and play at religion with this silly, empty-headed worship. I am not pleased" (Malachi 1:10).

If he were speaking directly to our culture today, I think he would say, "Put programs and bigness and your moral outrage where they belong—in second place. When they occupy first place in your heart, I find them detestable. I hate them.

"Can't you see the real battle going on in the human soul?

My people want something more than they want me. And it's ruining them.

⟲

Wake up! It's a heart problem. My people want something more than they want me. And it's ruining them. Their efforts to make life work are wearing them out and carrying them further and further from me. And I'm their only hope, their only source of rest and joy. Enter the battle. Learn to speak with power into people's lives. Arouse their desire for me until their thirst for me consumes them. When they get away with me, they'll recover their lives! The battle is for the heart. The battle is in the soul!"

ONE MAN'S STRUGGLE

Tim Burke is a friend of mine. After pitching in major league baseball with the New York Mets and the Minnesota Twins, he finished his all-star career with the New York Yankees. He retired early to spend more time with the five children he and Christine had adopted. *Major League Dad*, a book published by Focus on the Family, tells his remarkable story of love and sacrifice.[2]

The rest of the story, however, is not widely known. The four older children were each diagnosed with Reactive Attachment Disorder, a condition that, in their children's case, was severe enough to require long-term institutional care. Tim and Christine were devastated. Then the youngest, a sweet little girl born with half a left arm, suffered permanent brain damage during surgery when she was ten months old.

Tim reeled under the pressure. His faith took a beating, his marriage entered a dark tunnel, his financial resources were nearly exhausted, and for a long time Tim woke up every morning wishing he were dead. During his separation from his wife, Christine, he was pulled over for driving while intoxicated.

What battle was going on in Tim's soul? That question became personally important to me when God gave me the opportunity to meet with Tim for coffee-shop SoulTalk for two years.

Imagine that you're sitting down with Tim. Your heart goes out to him as he tells his story and shares his pain and failure. You're not sure what to say. Everything you think to say sounds simplistic, powerless, and cliché. You feel inadequate. You want to say something that will make a difference. You wish he were talking with Solomon. What do you do?

- Resist the urge to run!
- Resist the urge to help!
- Resist the urge to refer!

Think beneath. The life of God is in you. You long to speak that life into Tim's soul with power. But you have no idea what that means. You don't know what to say. Your natural tendency is to figure it out, to come up with the "right" words. Don't give in to that pressure. Direct your mind toward something else.

Think beneath more. You believe the life of the Spirit is in you; you believe he is moving. But where? Into what? What battle is going on in Tim's soul? That's the next thing to think about and to explore with Tim.

5

Go Beneath the Superficial

Entering the War Zone

We can and we must fight the real battle. But first we have to see it. And we must see the real battle clearly, in ourselves, then in others. If we don't, we'll patch up what we do see with band-aids, either religious or psychological. We'll become mere sentimentalists, dispensing reassuring theology that provides hope without foundation, or expert technicians who solve problems with models, methods, and programs.

But if we do see the battle, our mind will fill with passionate truth and our heart will burn with flaming love. We'll hear the rhythm of divine music, and we'll become dancing soldiers, warriors who liberate captives by speaking with powerful beauty into their lives.

In little pockets of community across the world, the Holy Spirit is opening the eyes of people who are desperate for reality, preparing us for war by letting us see what we're up against. His methods, as always, are surprising.

He's disillusioning us with all the exciting solutions to what we're now realizing are lesser battles—growing churches, funding programs, building families, fighting drugs, defending doctrine, strengthening friendships. Good and vital things, worthy objectives to pursue and to properly celebrate when achieved—but they aren't doing the job. They don't change us. We like the food, we feel nourished and happy, but we clean our plate and leave the table strangely hungry and still self-centered, unchanged on the inside, where it counts. The emptiness remains. And our soul cries for more. That cry is aroused by the Spirit!

Thanks to the same Spirit, we're becoming more frustrated with every formulaic strategy, whether a method of prayer or a set of principles, that promises to fill the void. Shallow solutions to bigger battles are losing their appeal. And the solutions that seemed so rich are being exposed as shallow. We're beginning to realize that the journey is not about getting our act together in prayer retreats or counseling sessions or anyplace else; it's about dropping our masks and facing the terror of living in a world without solutions to our biggest problems and then seeing that we belong in a different world. Then wholeness sneaks up on us.

We're waking up to a desire in our soul that nothing we experience is touching, not fully. If we stay honest in the middle of that awakening, a profound discontentment lets us see that the joy we're after is blocked by a subtle enemy that has long masqueraded as a friend. We thought it was a good thing to work on our marriage and advance our career and live to satisfy our desires for adventure and fulfillment and romance, and to do it all with priority energy. But by pursuing these good things as first things, we turn to God, if at all, only for cooperation, not for an experience of his presence. And we're seeing that such turning to God is not turning to God at all. It's telling him what to do, as a master would a servant.

It's becoming clear that our first order of business is not to pursue satisfaction, but to identify what's getting in the way of the deepest satisfaction available to the human soul. There's an enemy to recognize, a battle to engage. Our policy of containment isn't working. The Spirit is calling us to dance with him into the war zone, fully armed and prepared to destroy the enemy with grace, with spiritual power. It's time to enter the cosmic struggle taking place right now in our soul, with our mission clear and the victory we seek well defined and in sight.

Thanks to the Spirit, we want to. We want to enter the battle going on in our own soul and in the souls of those we love.

Now we need to know how. We first need to know what the battle is, and then, how to fight it.

RECOGNIZE THE REAL BATTLE

You're sitting across from Tim. You're hearing his story. You're feeling overwhelmed. For a moment, you sense how much you'd prefer to be playing golf or listening to a success story of how God has worked. You *don't* want to hear how bad things are. It evokes a quiet terror in you. Something like that could happen to you. And as you listen, you really don't know what to say.

hard not to *think escape*, to avoid running away into plati-
tudes, cheap prayer, or easy kindness. And it's hard not to *think
help*, to resist the urge to pursue a master's in counseling or
extensive training in spiritual direction in hopes of escaping
that terrible feeling of inadequacy. It's not easy to recognize
your inadequacy as an opportunity to hear the rhythm of the
Spirit in your soul.

It's hard not to *think referral*, to keep from telling yourself, "I'm
in way over my head. I can be a friend to Tim, but he needs to
be talking with someone who's trained to handle this kind of
thing. I mean, this is serious stuff. He's really depressed."

But don't *think escape* or *think help* and don't too quickly *think
referral*. Certainly you'll feel like running. You'll want to help.
And it's true that referral to a physician for medication (if
nothing else, to let Tim sleep) or to a seasoned counselor for
wisdom you don't have might be appropriate. But don't under-
estimate your power to speak into Tim's life. We *thought beneath*
in chapter 3 to see the supernatural life that's already in us, and
there's no greater power.

So, believing that God's power is in you (though you don't
yet feel it and won't till you're in the middle of the battle and
apparently losing), and thinking beneath to acknowledge that
the literal life of God is right now flowing through your soul,
the next step is to *think beneath* to the battle. Beneath every one of
Tim's shattered dreams, beneath every ounce of pain that
unavoidably accompanies the terrible events in his life, there is
a battle being fought that you are equipped to enter. And it is
the most important battle in Tim's life.

It will do no good to hear me describe the battle and for you to say, "Oh, that! Yes, that's the spiritual dimension of the problem." We will not speak into anyone's life with supernatural power until we see the battle, until we are silenced into humility, until we have nothing to say, until we fall to our knees and cry out, "Father, hallowed be your name. Lead us not into temptation, but deliver us from evil. God, have mercy! Without you, we're all dead."

Bear with me. I need two chapters, this one and the next, to adjust the focus till the battle comes clearly into sight. Three truths will help us stay present, with patient discernment, long enough to see what must be seen.

We will not speak into anyone's life with supernatural power until we see the battle.

TRUTH #1: SOULTALK INVOLVES AUTHENTIC ENCOUNTER

SoulTalk, the weapon you'll need once you see the battle, is not a scientific technique practiced by a skilled expert. It's the language people speak when the life in them meets the need in others (see Ephesians 4:29).

The key is authentic encounter, not professional precision. SoulTalk is not surgery. It does not remove something bad or repair something damaged. It's more like consummation. It pours something alive into the fertile soul of another.

And when that happens, when others sense that you are

speaking life and wanting to speak it into them, the wall around their soul weakens. It begins to crumble—not always, but often; not fully, but a little. It happened when Jesus spoke to the woman at the well. "You want to give me *living* water? I'm listening."

That's the first truth: You are supernaturally alive, so you can speak with supernatural power into your kids, your spouse, your friends, your counselee. Remember that, and you will want to see the real battle, because you will feel energized by the prospect of speaking into it.

TRUTH #2: SOULTALK REQUIRES COMMUNION WITH THE TRINITY

SoulTalk happens when your heart is right, when you're in communion with the Trinity.

We don't usually speak SoulTalk to each other. But not because we lack knowledge or skill, though we may. We lack rhythm—or, more precisely, we aren't feeling the rhythm that's in us.

Heather could demonstrate the movements of the foxtrot for an hour. She could diagram it on a chalkboard with masterful accuracy. But if I don't feel the rhythm and give myself to it, if something alive in me doesn't hear the music's beat, I'll never dance.

The rhythm is already in me. The divine fountain could be gushing up out of my soul, moving gracefully in rhythm with the song of delight that the Father is singing over me. And yet

I speak SelfTalk. Why? Why aren't I dancing? Why aren't I speaking with power into your life?

Answer? I'm moving to the wrong tune. The energy flowing out of me is not divine water; it's natural sewage. And it's swaying with the proud, terrified beat of a soul determined to prove itself, to win attention, to gain approval, to feel important, to be seen as powerful, to protect itself, to exercise enough control to make life work for me, whatever that might mean.

When I first met Tim, I was impressed, a little star-struck. Thousands of people paid big bucks to watch this guy throw baseballs in big league stadiums. He wore Yankee pinstripes, the same pinstripes that Joe DiMaggio, Mickey Mantle, and Casey Stengel wore. And there he was, sitting across from me in the coffee shop, pouring out his heart to me.

I wanted to do good, to let him know that, though I may not be the athlete he is, I can do *my* thing pretty well. I can throw words right down the middle, to the left up high or to the right down low, change-ups, sliders, fastballs, whatever gets the job done. When it comes to SoulTalk, just watch. I'm the all-star!

So I had to perform. Pressure mounted. Fear cast out love. I said things to impress him and liked it when he swung and missed, when I blew a thought right by him that he didn't get. I wasn't even thinking about the battle Tim was fighting. I was too busy fighting a silly battle of my own.

I listened to the screams of hell and thought it was music. My natural energy was more concerned to prove something about me than to reveal something about God. And the world's tune, inspired by the devil, directed the arrhythmic dance.

That's not mere silliness; it's evil. There are seven things the Lord hates, and pride tops the list (see Proverbs 6:16–19). My heart was out of sync with God. I was more concerned with me than with God. I couldn't hear heaven's music. I couldn't speak SoulTalk.

But when I identified my sinful agendas, when I could see how clumsily and damagingly I was moving into my friend's life, I heard a different tune. It was quiet at first. But as I inclined my ear, the music became louder. And it was beautiful.

It was the Father's song of delight, over me, *right then,* composed by the Son, sung by the Spirit: "This isn't what you want to do. It doesn't reflect who you are. You're a better man than that. I know. I made you a better man. Don't hide. It's all taken care of. You're forgiven. Listen to your heart. That's my home. That's where I live. You long to hear your friend, to see the battle he's fighting and to pour into him the life I have poured into you. I love you. I am delighted to be with you. I enjoy you. You love me. And you love Tim. Go, speak with him."

That's when I started dancing. A strange image, a dancing soldier, but that's what I became. Like Jesus. It's what happened on the cross. He defeated sin by releasing his whole being to move in rhythm with the Father's will. He danced into battle and won.

And it happened in the coffee shop, off and on with Tim for two years. When our heart is in tune with heaven's music, when agonizing shame and brokenness open our ears to hear the music, then we dance into battle.

Remember that, and you'll move with grace to find yourself in the heat of the battle.

TRUTH #3: SOULTALK WAITS FOR THE SPIRIT

SoulTalk waits. It is patient. We don't set the timetable for change. That's the Spirit's work. The pressure's off. We can relax.

When our sons were six and eight, I decided one night at supper that it was time for them to get serious about God. Earlier that afternoon, I had received word that a spiritual mentor from graduate school days had jettisoned the faith. It shook me to the core. If it happened to him, it could happen to anyone, including my kids.

So I mounted my steed, drew my sword, and charged into battle. Surely it was God's will that my boys surrender fully to Christ, *that* night. After a stirring devotional from God's Word, I turned to my sons, wagged my finger in their bewildered faces, and with crusade fervor declared, "You two *will* live for God! Is that clear?"

I've had better moments. That was nothing but SelfTalk, rank and offensive. When the stakes are high, it's severely tempting to take matters into our own hands, to let a spirit of necessity rule within us, to assume control over what we can never control, another person's soul. How foolish. How arrogant. It's idolatrous. And it produces nothing but SelfTalk—many "right" words, but none with a drop of the Spirit's power.

Remember that, and as you speak with Tim, you'll wait, you'll listen, you'll care, and you'll pray. You'll patiently *think beneath.* Perhaps God will reveal the battle and let you speak with power into it. Maybe he'll work a miracle right before your eyes today. Maybe he won't. It's not your call. It's his.

MOVE TO THE CENTER OF THE BATTLE

With these three truths in mind, listen now to a few words from a dancing soldier, a man who spent years entering the battle for people's souls with supernatural power. Here's what he said: "Be prepared. You're up against far more than you can handle on your own. Take all the help you can get, every weapon God has issued, so that when it's all over but the shouting you'll still be on your feet. . . . Pray hard and long. . . . Keep your eyes open" (Ephesians 6:13, 18).

We have our marching orders from the apostle Paul. Let's go to war!

Move right to the center of the battle. Ask yourself the key question: What does Tim want most? To be closer to God and more like his Son? Or something else?

Ask the same question differently, again to yourself, not out loud. Is the person you're speaking with more interested in *communion* with God that will satisfy his soul or in *cooperation* from God that will improve his life and a *convenient* plan he can follow that will bring it about?

When life is hard, the most natural thing in the world is to want relief, to want the difficulties to ease up and a few things to go our way. When life is going well, the most natural thing in the world is to want whatever's going well to continue going well. And in both cases, we'd prefer to be aware of something we can do that would increase the odds of gaining relief or keeping blessings. Dependence on another has never proved reliable. Independence, self-sufficiency, is a much better plan. That's the natural way to think.

Whether life is bumpy or smooth, the most supernatural thing we can do is to want to know God better, to value his pleasure and his purposes above everything else, and to want directions for the journey into his presence more than a plan for making life work. Of course Tim wanted his life to improve. That's not sinful or wrong. It's normal. The question is, Did he want God more?

Whether life is bumpy or smooth, the most supernatural thing we can do is to want to know God better.

Abraham wanted his son to live, but he wanted to know God more. Mary wanted to avoid the humiliation of a pregnancy before marriage, but she wanted to surrender to God more. Jesus wanted to avoid the experience of being treated like a sinner by his Father, but he wanted to please him more.

Adam wanted to stay in communion with God. But he wanted what he perceived to be the advantages of control more. And with that choice, Adam brought the fiercest battle being raged, between Satan and God, into human experience.

And that's the battle, the battle of competing desires. That's the war zone, where things that we legitimately want become more important than knowing and trusting and following God, and where the pleasures that we experience when things in life go well feel more intense and are therefore more desired than the pleasure of experiencing God himself. The Bible calls it idolatry.

Tim is hurting. He feels despair. He doesn't want to go on living. Memories of fans cheering, the excited anticipation of signing adoption papers, and his former closeness to his lovely wife torture him. If he could turn back the clock, he would. He can see nothing ahead but darkness and more pain. Why go on?

If someone came up with a plan to straighten out his kids, to restore intimacy in his marriage, to feel valuable and competent and appreciated again, Tim would jump at it. Who wouldn't? If fasting would persuade God to bring back the blessings, if spiritual direction would help him develop more patience and feel more peace until things got better, if participation in a small group or serving on a ministry team or going away with guys on a fly-fishing trip would improve his outlook, he'd get involved.

Lodged deep in his soul is the basic agenda of Adam's children: *I want to do something that will make my life better.*

Lodged deeper in his soul is the basic agenda of God's children: *I want to experience God through whatever means he provides and keep trusting him whether life gets better or not.*

The battle is on. Natural desire demands first place, yet supernatural desire won't budge. Let's take a closer look at the battle, until we kneel and pray.

6

MOVE IN FOR A CLOSER LOOK

Recognizing Religion As the Real Enemy

RELIGION IS THE INVENTION OF THE DEVIL. The world has taken out the patent. We humans have mortgaged our souls to buy the product, and we think we've gotten a good deal. "Religion is the most dangerous energy source known to humankind," says Eugene Peterson in his introduction to the prophecy of Amos in *The Message*.

In the aftermath of World War II, politicians campaigned on their vision of prosperity: two cars in every garage, a chicken in every pot. Since Eden, the devil's landslide victory—he's won every vote but one—has been carried by the slogan "Religion in every soul." His message was enticing. Live smart. Your life can work. Unlike the politicians, he's produced. Or at least he's made it look as though he has.

Thanks to Satan, we all enter life with a proud, natural passion. It's his legacy to us, through Adam. We want to do something to make our life better. The theology of religion can be expressed in a simple tenet: *The effort to harness whatever power is available in the service of whatever goal we value is a right and noble endeavor.*

Moral religion, of course, stipulates that the pursuit of our goal must not violate others' pursuit of their goal. More generally, making life better for yourself, and for others if you can, is the idea. That's religion. It leaves narcissism, a core commitment to our own well-being above all other values, firmly in place.

Satan has made good on his platform. Religion, the self-absorbed search for a way to be in control of our own well-being, is now the natural energy in every human soul. And it's killing us. We were made for the spiritual journey. We're walking the religious journey, and it's responsible for everything we call nonorganic psychological disorder. It robs us of joy while promising an overflow. Even when it seems to work, it's wearing us out or puffing us up.

What does Jesus see when he looks at Tim, when he sees into you or me? Once he stood before a large crowd and saw people who were "harassed and helpless" (Matthew 9:36 NIV), even though, in all probability, they looked like they had their act together. The words could be translated *pressured* and *weary.* Jesus saw a battle raging in their souls, between following Satan and following God. Religion, Satan's invention, was winning. Everyone was working hard to meet whatever requirements they thought were necessary for life to go well, and they were bone-weary with the effort.

Do this! Do that! Protect yourself. Look out for your own

well-being. Here's the way to live, to make your kids behave, to make your church grow, to make your depression lift. Be nice to people, be patient and kind. C'mon, you can do it. Get busy! Work harder! Keep trying! You'll get it. *And your life will work!*

Those were the lyrics to the music the Pharisees played. We sing the same song today, in our families, in our schools, in our businesses, and too often in our churches. Are your kids breaking your heart? Deal with them God's way. Is money a problem? Here are biblical principles of finances. Lonely? Angry? Irritable? Depressed? Bothered by terrible memories? Let me explain what's going on and how you can fix things. It's all religion. It's all SelfTalk.

THE BATTLE BEGINS

An epidemic is often best understood by tracing all cases back to the first. As Jesus looked out on the Galileans years ago and looks into us today, I imagine his mind not only going way beneath the superficial, but also going back in time, to when the battle began, when religion first appeared.

A beautiful, blessed, and happy angel of God somehow got it in his head that something might actually bring him more pleasure than revolving his life around God. Felt desire became more central to his allegiance than God's person. Apparently he wanted the perks of deity—total authority, personal control over everything, worship—and he decided to go after them.

The treasonous pursuit of ultimate pleasure apart from subordinate intimacy with God took over his will. Lucifer lost touch with reality and became Satan, the first moral psychotic. There *is* no ultimate pleasure apart from God, but he thought there was.

Lucifer went mad but never became stupid. With unrivaled cunning, he pulled off the biggest scam in history. He convinced creatures who were designed to enjoy love from God and to love God and others in return that there was something better: control. Personal desire became central. We were blinded to the fact that our deepest desires would be fully satisfied only in the presence of God's glory, with him in the center. We became fools, like our religious father.

The disease of religion was introduced into the human soul. I experience its symptoms every day. Getting my wife to treat me in a certain way can seem more satisfying than treating her in a certain way. Impressing Tim can feel more pleasurable than serving Tim. The battle is on.

As Adam's child, I want control. I want to be able to arrange for my well-being as I see fit. And I think God, or whomever I decide to trust, should cooperate.

As God's child, I want him. I want to experience communion with him as authentically as I experience sexual pleasure with my wife, only more so, deeper, more satisfying to my soul. Somehow I know that no pleasure—physical, personal, or relational—can match the joys of knowing God. I want to trust him, looking forward to knowing him better, no matter what else happens.

Natural desire competes with supernatural desire. The pleasures of life vie for first place with the pleasures of God. Religion and Christianity are at war.

Israel's history provides a clear picture of the battle. A man named Jeroboam led a rebellion against the rightful but greedy king of Israel. He formed a separate nation that became known as the northern kingdom.

But there was one hitch. Jerusalem was in the original land, the southern kingdom, and King Jeroboam feared that his subjects would want to worship there, as they had been told by God to do.

So Jeroboam made worship easy. With devilish wisdom, he subtly replaced Jehovah worship with religion. At one end of his country, in a city called Dan, he erected a golden calf, representing God. At the other end, in Bethel, he put another one, to save his people the trouble of traveling so far to worship and to protect against his followers returning to the other kingdom. "It is too much for you to go up to Jerusalem," he told his people. "Here are your gods, O Israel" (1 Kings 12:28 NIV).

The pleasures of life vie for first place with the pleasures of God.

It's important to realize what Jeroboam did. *He made God convenient,* for his own purposes. The God of glory became a convenient god who offered a religious plan everyone could follow, telling his people, "Just do this. You'll be fine."

Years later, under Ahab and Jezebel, Baal worship was introduced to Israel. Baal was the god of agricultural fertility, a cooperative god who said, "Indulge your desires" and supplied temple prostitutes so men could find easy pleasure in worship. Baal promised, "I'll see to it that things go well for you—abundant crops, overflowing banquet tables, great parties."

The *god of convenience* combined with the *god of cooperation* to produce a most satisfying religion.

THE MESSAGE OF RELIGION

As I look over the Western church, and as I look into my own heart, I hear the message of religion: *Get it reasonably right, and life will go reasonably well.* When I follow my religious (versus spiritual) impulses, I either feel smugly confident or angrily defeated. In both cases, pride and fear lay at the center. Either my life is full of wonderful blessings and I believe I have the inside track on God's favor because I'm living acceptably, or things are tough and I'm mad at God because I thought I was doing pretty well and mad at myself for missing the mark.

Reflect on the summary sketch that follows. See if you can recognize this way of thinking in your own soul.

> *The god of convenience:*
> *Get it reasonably right*
> plus
> *The god of cooperation:*
> *Life will work reasonably well*
> equals
> *Religion: You can make your life work in a way*
> *that satisfies your soul.*

If that kind of thinking is going on in Tim's soul, it needs to be defeated and replaced with a very different understanding of life.

Notice first that the incentive driving religion is not communion with God; it is the blessings of life. We believe Satan's lie that there really is something to be treasured above knowing God, becoming like Jesus, and abandoning ourselves to the Spirit. Enjoy whatever your experience tells you will bring the richest pleasure to your soul. That's how religion defines life.

For Tim, at one time that meant sacrificing fame and fortune to adopt five kids with dreams of celebrating happy family times around the Christmas tree and watching God restore the lives of troubled children. Had his dreams come true, Tim might today be a contented religious man.

When things fell apart, he became a defeated religious man, still believing something should work to bring him life but now convinced it would never happen.

Tim is now an imperfect but growing spiritual man, for one big reason: He has rejected the devil's lie that life consists of making things work and now believes that life is all about knowing God better, no matter the cost, and moving into the challenges of life to further God's purposes, not his. He's not arrived, but he's on the spiritual, not the religious, journey.

With the devil, the flesh within us says, "Real life is the enjoyment of blessings in this world, which God (or fate) gives to those who get it right." With Christ, the Spirit within us says, "Real life consists in dependence on God, clinging to him when everything goes wrong, tramping down despair with the weight of the Cross, and waiting on the Spirit to draw us nearer into the Father's heart, doing all that we can to create space for the Spirit to work."

THE BATTLE OF COMPETING DESIRES

Now we can more clearly recognize the real battle going on in our soul, what I earlier called the battle of competing desires.

Every follower of Jesus has two sets of desires: the desire to know God and to experience intimate communion with the Trinity, and the desire to hear the specific calling of the Spirit in our life, to be so anchored in the hope of eternal joy and to be so in love with Jesus now that we endure every hardship as a privilege and as an opportunity to become more like Christ.

That's in us. It's in me. It's in you. It's in Tim. But there's something else: We want this life to go well. We long to feel a certain way; to handle tough situations in commendable fashion; to become a friendly, good, uncomplaining person; to enjoy at least a measure of success in whatever matters to us; to be noticed and wanted; to feel personal value and worth; to experience the pleasure of good family, good friendships, good health, good income, and good ministry; to feel less stress and more peace, less emptiness and more joy.

Both sets of desires are legitimate. We must understand that. Never think of yourself as unspiritual because you hurt over lost blessings and pray fervently for restored blessings. Of course you want to feel good. That's how you were designed by God.

The battle begins when the desire for blessings in life becomes the ruling passion of our heart. It's happened in all of us, beginning at birth. It's the driving force of religion. You want that? Good! Here's how to get it. And when you get it, you'll experience life.

Jesus taught that the core longing of our soul is the desire to know God, not the desire to feel loved, not the desire to experience meaning, not the desire for the pleasures of family, friends, or success, but the passion to know God as high and lifted up and to place ourselves beneath him, resting in his goodness and available for his purposes.

Call that the "first-thing" desire. Call every other longing of the heart "second-thing" desires. When each desire is in place, we are spiritual people, not religious.

But that never happens, not fully, till heaven. It's always a struggle to honor our desire for knowing God as absolutely primary and to genuinely regard every other desire as secondary. The *central battle* in the souls of Jesus followers is the battle to keep the first-thing desire in first place and second-thing desires in second place.

> The *central battle* in the souls of Jesus followers is the battle to keep the first-thing desire in first place and second-thing desires in second place.

The *central evil* in the human soul is the natural tendency to elevate second-thing desires to first place and to pursue their satisfaction as if the well-being of our soul depended on it.

The *central deception* in every soul is to believe that second-thing desires belong in first place, to be deeply convinced that the core well-being of our soul does in fact depend on their satisfaction.

And the *central point* of SoulTalk is to awaken and nourish the first-thing desire until the passion for God becomes consuming, the ruling passion of the soul, stronger than every other desire. That is spiritual formation.

When someone shares a journeying reality, a part of his or her experience that person feels safe in making known to you, don't run, don't try to fix anything, and don't quickly refer. Instead, *think beneath.* The following sketch depicts what I've been saying.

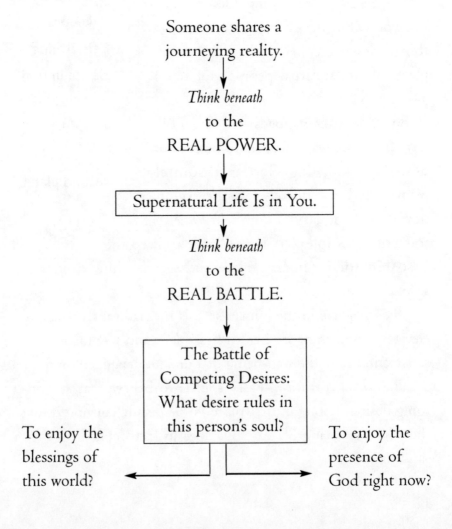

Before we shift our attention to the next element in SoulTalk, let's remember a few things.

First, God has not promised us a better life of blessings in this world. Blessings may come to faithful people. They may not come to faithful people. Rain falls on the godly and the ungodly. So does hail. There is no linear relationship between getting it reasonably right and having life go reasonably well. That's the lie of religion.

Second, what Paul called the Old Way of the written code (see Romans 7:6; Deuteronomy 29:9; and Hebrews 7:18–19)[1] is a weakened and corrupted version of God's Old Covenant with his people. He required absolute perfection, a careful keeping of the entire law, as the condition for deserved blessings. None of us qualified. Religion, as opposed to the Old Covenant, reduces God to a convenient and cooperative deity, makes obedience easy by requiring only what we can do, and then promises a pleasant life if we at least try hard. Get it reasonably right and life will work reasonably well. That's the Old Way. That's religion, and it turns prayer into presumption, worship into negotiation, and obedience into pressure.

Finally, when we speak with people in an effort to help them live better so their life works better, we offer life management, not SoulCare, and we speak SelfTalk. When we join people on their journey away from religion toward Christianity, into the New Way of the Spirit who leads us to God, we offer SoulCare, and we speak SoulTalk.

THE BATTLE IN TIM'S SOUL

The battle in Tim's soul boils down to this: The desire for things to go better so he can feel better feels like the strongest, most unmet and reasonable longing in his soul. And he is willing to do whatever it takes for that to happen. His willingness seems to him to evidence humility and surrender. In fact it's a demand, fueled by a spirit of entitlement. His soul has been drawn into the wrong path. Tim is religious. His anger and depression seem justified.

Tim doesn't yet know it, but a desire to know God and to trust God with his current and eternal well-being is planted deeply in his soul. He yearns to experience communion with the Trinity and, if his yearning was richly felt, he would see every heartache in life as an opportunity to know God better and to reveal Christ to whoever's watching. And that would thrill his soul. He would still hurt, but with hope, even joy.

Two desires. Each one claims first place. One is a usurper. When second-thing desires rule, they become demands. Then Tim's self-centeredness rules, beneath all the pain. When first-thing desire rules, when the desire for God is rightfully on the throne, it is experienced as an earnest, passionate, mercy-dependent yearning of the heart. Then Tim begins to resemble Jesus.

Which desire will rule his life? The opposing armies are fighting. The war is on. It's the same battle in all of us.

Now with an awareness of the life in us and the battle in another, let's imagine what the Spirit can do. Let's *think vision*. It's the next lesson in SoulTalk.

7

Go After the Very Best

Seeing a Vision of True Goodness

Two friends were sitting in our living room one evening. We talked for several hours. The day before, the man had confessed to moral failure. His wife was numb. Shelli, their teenage daughter, was home with a friend.

"Honey, I am *so* sorry. I've hurt you so bad. I will never be unfaithful to you again. I promise. I told Shelli just this afternoon how much I love you, that if I had it to do all over again, I'd pick you for my wife in a heartbeat. Please! *Please* forgive me!"

Each word was spoken with throbbing emotion. When he finished, he buried his face in his hands and sobbed. His wife was unmoved. So was I. It all sounded so religious.

I sat quietly. What should I say? Did I have any power? To accomplish what? These were my friends. I loved them. And I wanted to see their marriage work. What should I do?

Do I assure the sinning husband of grace? Treat him for

sexual addiction? Make sure he faces the ugliness of his sin to provoke deeper repentance?

Do I gently explore what his wife is feeling, what she's thinking, what her plans are? Do I wonder what unhealed wounds this current abuse is touching in her?

Do I tell him his words felt more to me like a canned speech than deep repentance? More self-focused than God-focused? Partly manipulative and therefore capable of turning angry if his purposes are blocked? Do I applaud his courage in confessing before he was caught and point it out to his wife as a hopeful sign? Do I nudge him to notice her stony response to his pleas and to wonder what's going on in her? Do I look for basic struggles in his feeling manly and in her feeling womanly, then identify longstanding wounds still attached to tough memories in each of them and introduce the gospel's power to heal wounds and to correct deeply embedded lies that they might both still believe?

What should I say?

WHAT SHOULD I SAY?

That question is the most natural question to ask when talking with a troubled friend. It is also the least useful and the most dangerous. No single question has interfered more than this one with the release of loving, powerful, wise, and graceful spiritual rhythm. Asking it leads naturally to introducing clumsy religion into the conversation, things like approved interventions, strict accountability, clever interpretations, step-by-step procedures for healing, or the mechanical application of biblical principles.

Asking it is like asking whether to turn left or right at the dead end without knowing where you want to go. Or worse, deciding which turn to take with a destination in mind that you think will provide water to quench your thirst but in fact will carry you farther into the desert.

If we're headed where the Spirit is going, toward the only place of true goodness, then we'll develop a reliable sense of spiritual direction. We'll see his light, we'll hear his voice, we'll recognize his wisdom from the Scripture, and we'll know what to say. Instead of asking, "What should I say?" we'll ask, "Am I following the Spirit to the good place I see?" We'll make mistakes. We'll move off course. But we'll realize it and listen more closely. We'll hear heaven's music, we'll feel the rhythm, and we'll dance into battle.

It all depends on following the Spirit to his goal. To do that, we need to *think vision.* If we head somewhere else, we'll be on our own. We'll feel ourselves scrambling, trying to decide if now is the time for empathy or confrontation, for focusing on a solution or probing for answers. Our scrambling might defensively end in complacent professionalism—we might adopt one theoretical model, become proficient in its practice, and move boldly into the fray with proud self-confidence, either as therapists or spiritual directors.

Without a God-centered, Jesus-honoring, Spirit-inspired vision, we'll speak SelfTalk. It happens all the time. The enemy of our souls disguises himself as a light-providing angel and persuades us that second-thing desires are legitimate goals: Heal their wounds, improve their communication, get him accountable to his community and proud of it, make accountability the source of his confidence in staying away from further failure, soften her into giving him another chance, and pay no attention when she sees her "forgiveness" as a noble gesture.

For Satan, any vision will do except the vision of wanting God above all else, at any cost, letting every chip fall where it may; any vision except valuing God so greatly that nothing matters more than revealing what he's like, than becoming like Jesus, than yielding to the rule of the Spirit within us.

If desiring God was our vision, we'd speak SoulTalk. Supernatural life would pour out of our soul into our friends. We wouldn't crouch behind the bunker, wondering what maneuvers would take us successfully into battle. We'd hear the music, we'd feel the rhythm, and we'd dance over the bunker into battle, away from the wall and onto the dance floor. We'd move with the freedom of authenticity in the liberty of the Spirit. Life would flow from our depths, carry our words, and shape their selection. We'd speak quietly, sometimes loudly, either way with real power, always kindly, and with genuine love and wise timing.

So the better question is not, "What should I say?" but, "What is my vision?" Let's think about that. Let's *think vision*, the second element in SoulTalk.

THINK VISION

Perhaps the first thing to realize is that at every moment, in every conversation, we already have a vision. We want something to happen, and we're already committed to doing whatever we think will get us there. We have a vision for *ourselves*, and we have a vision for *others*. Focus with me on the vision we have for others: What do we most want to see happen in others as we hear them share their journey?

Put yourself in my living room, talking with a couple whose pain breaks your heart, with a husband whose failure makes you hate sin and resolve to live more purely, with a wife whose devastation brings back memories of your own. What's your vision? What was mine as I sat with them?

Is our highest vision for this couple a restored marriage? If so, we're putting second things first. The devil has tricked us. We're wanting a good thing but mistaking it for the best thing, from which every other good thing flows.

A priority vision for a restored marriage is a religious vision, and it calls us to provide religious direction, to figure out what we must do to help put this marriage together and to understand what each spouse must do to restore trust and intimacy to their relationship. Together we feel pressed to get it right, and we soon become weary with the effort.

Envisioning nothing greater than a good marriage puts the focus on the wrong question. It makes us ask what we should say. So we listen for instructions and fail to hear the music that could get us dancing. We try to get it right and, in the process, move perhaps with professional precision but with little relational rhythm. Our internal barometer is ignored. The Spirit is quenched as we sincerely try to help.

But suppose our vision was not a restored marriage, but two restored souls. Then we'd turn away from those who would offer us only principles and move instead toward our dance instructor, the Holy Spirit. With spiritual vision replacing religious vision, we'd hear the music play, we'd follow our teacher onto the dance floor into the hearts of our friends, and we'd provide spiritual direction. We'd dance with our friends into the presence of God, not easily, often clumsily, but we would be following the Spirit toward his vision. It might take awhile. We're not very good dancers, and neither are our friends. But moving together toward a spiritual vision gives their marriage its best chance. As C. S. Lewis wrote, "You can't get second things by putting them first; you can get second things only by putting first things first."[1]

Do you see it? The Old Way of religion says:

Figure out what needs to be done to put this marriage together. That's a *good* thing, right? Do whatever it takes. Draw from biblical principles, use counseling theory, employ relational techniques. Teach the steps to forgiveness and instruct them in communication skills, anger management strategies, approaches to conflict resolution.

Treat sexual addiction according to the latest methodologies, build self-esteem with assurances of grace, encourage the discovery and release of true manhood and womanhood. Exhort both spouses to fight for their marriage, not to give up, to hate divorce as much as God does, to study Scripture to determine if there are biblical grounds for divorce present in this marriage.

Pursue no higher value than obedience to the Bible (get it

reasonably right) and expect that God will either restore the marriage or strengthen them to rebuild their lives (life will work reasonably well).

Religion encourages us to be preoccupied with the *fruits* of knowing God, not with the *reality*, to be a religious friend, to embrace the Old Way vision of a good life. But when we do, we speak SelfTalk. Results may seem good, but the conversation will move no one closer to true goodness. Second things are in first place. The path may seem right, but its end is the absence of all goodness. God has been replaced as the object of our affections. He has instead become the means to what we most want.

The New Way of the Spirit is entirely different. Listen to its message:

Everything needed to draw near to God is in place. The husband is fully forgiven by God. His identity, in God's eyes, is Jesus follower, not adulterer or sex addict. His deepest longing is not to feel alive as a man or to win his wife back; it's to know and enjoy God, to reveal God by becoming more like Jesus. And he has all the power he needs to move toward that vision. He does not have the power to change his wife's heart. That's between her and God's Spirit.

And his wife, though deeply and legitimately hurt, is at the moment more committed to protecting herself against further hurt than to knowing God. Yet even in that condition of soul, because of the gospel, she is whole as a woman and profoundly beautiful. God delights in her. Her idolatrous determination never to hurt like this again is fully forgiven. It is not understood by an empathic God as much as it is forgiven by a holy and gracious God. Her identity is not an adulterer's wife. She is a saint who is flawed and hurting, married to a flawed and hurting brother in Christ who has betrayed her trust.

Her deepest, most passionate desire (though she cannot feel it at the moment) is to walk through her misery into the presence of God. It is not to close the door and run away. The Spirit has made no promise to supply the power to keep her soul safe from further hurt in her marriage. If that is her vision, she will be on her own, and personal safety will be her vision—*unless her appetite for God is aroused.* The Spirit will supply the power to wrap her soul around God, if that's what she most wants.

A vision to know God better will come into focus as her desire to know God is awakened. Her pain and fear will continue, but she will begin to experience peace and joy. And she will quietly come alive with the power to forgive and the wisdom to make God-honoring decisions that reveal the character of God to her husband, her daughter, and her friends. Eventually, that will mean more to her than protecting herself from further pain or relieving the pain that's already there.

LEARNING TO DANCE WITH THE SPIRIT

Back to the living room. We're ten minutes into the conversation. The man is sobbing. The woman stiffens. What do we say? Answer: We ask a different question. We ask, "Where are we heading?" What do we most yearn to see happen as we enter the battle for their souls?

Do we even recognize the real battle? Do we see that so much more is at stake than whether this couple gets back together? It's so natural to want to make sense of things, to reduce God to being convenient and cooperative, to figure out what we can do to make this marriage work, to be powerful helpers.

But that's wrong. When our second-thing desire to see their marriage restored, or even to see their souls restored, ascends to first place in our heart, we instantly become religious. We cease worshiping God and look instead for a way to use him. That's *our* battle.

And *their* battle is similar. Of course the husband wants his wife to forgive him. Of course he wants to become accountable to friends, to enter community as never before. Of course he wants to enjoy a happy home with his wife and daughter and to do whatever is required to make that happen.

Of course his wife doesn't want to hurt ever again like she hurts now. Of course she is scared and wants to trust her husband only if he becomes trustworthy. Of course she would love to have a happy Christmas morning with mom, dad, and daughter opening presents together; but if he won't change, she doesn't want him there.

There's no sin in any of that for either of them, unless those desires assume life-and-death status, unless they can think of nothing more wonderful, nothing more necessary to their souls' well-being than the fulfillment of all these understandable and healthy desires.

And that's *their* battle. Of course they desire to enjoy life. But when second-thing desires assume first place in their affections, they reduce God to a pawn in their plans. They try to figure out what to do that will make their lives better; they assume they are entitled to something going well so they can live and not die. What an affront to Christ, who is their life.

All the while, the Spirit continues to whisper, to play soft music, to shine a light into their darkness. And we, their friends, dance to the music. "Religion will kill you," the Spirit says. "You'll never get it right enough to deserve blessing. But Jesus has made a way to the highest blessing. He's opened a way to the better hope, to true goodness, to enter the presence of God and to rest in his love and power. Draw near to him, and he will draw near to you."

The man is still sobbing. The woman continues to stiffen. We *think battle*. And we *think vision*.

The man looks up, expecting his sobs will provoke some response from us, perhaps a reassuring smile, maybe a gesture of support. The woman glances our way, wondering if perhaps we have no idea what to do and feel unable to cope with this level of marital mess; or maybe she thinks we're just disgusted with the whole thing and wish we were somewhere else.

We resist their pull to speak just yet. Our silence surprises them. For a few minutes, maybe longer, they worry that we're incompetent, ill-equipped for problems like these. But soon a strange dynamic occurs. They realize they have no power over us. And they begin to feel *safe*.

We don't jump to handle their pain. We don't try to fix

anything or make anything better. We're listening to another voice, focusing our eyes to see what's invisible but more real than everything the natural eye can see. Our soul is resting in the Father's authority, our hope is fixed on Christ, our ears are tuned to hear the Spirit.

We *think battle* and are eager to fight. We *think vision* and are trembling with excitement. The stage is being set. We're about to speak, not with extraordinary brilliance or impressive skill, but with ordinary words, simple words, words that aim toward the New Way vision, words such as, "You've hurt your wife far more with your shallow passion for God than with your moral failure." We turn to her and say, "The pain that you're feeling is opening your soul to experience your deepest desire."

We feel God's life flowing through our words. We know where we're headed, and it's good. The dance is under way.

But neither of them moves with us. Even when we *think beneath*, see the real battle, and enter it; even when we *think vision* and imagine what it would mean for the people sitting with us to value God as their supreme treasure, nothing happens, at least nothing visible.

Another dancing warrior has written, "Anyone who has entered the darkness of another's pain, loss, or bewilderment, and who has done so without the defenses of a detached professionalism, will know the feeling of wanting to escape, of wishing they had not become involved."[2]

It's hard to dance without a partner. It's discouraging to lead in a direction and have no one follow. But when it happens, we have the opportunity to become detached from our second-thing desire for visible results that affirm our value, and to become more attached to the first thing—wanting to know and honor and reveal God as the deepest hope of the soul, even if the couple walks out and never returns.

And that centers us. We relax. We love more deeply. The pressure falls off. When we speak again, the struggle to convince them to walk with us is less. We get out of the Holy Spirit's way and simply speak the truth in love.

We rest in God while at the same time our heart yearns for our friends to rest in God. Knowing him becomes the greatest good we can imagine for them. Our vision becomes clearer, more appealing than ever.

THE RIGHT TIME

The timing is right to develop the New Way vision, to leave the religious path and begin walking the spiritual journey, to value the presence of God more than the blessings of life.

A fresh wind from the Spirit is blowing in the souls of people across the world. We're waking up to the hunger in our soul for more than a life that goes well, we're feeling boredom with everything less than the experience of his presence, we're realizing we'll never feel now all we were designed to feel and will only feel in heaven.

And we're seeing that much of the "new spirituality" of our day is freshly packaged religion, a "revival of self-cultivation, where all the emphasis is on personal growth, a spirituality which is self-centered rather than God-centered."[3]

Augustine's words are resonating: "There can be only two basic loves, the love of God unto the forgetfulness of self, or the love of self unto the forgetfulness of God."[4]

When we hear those words, the demons gnash their teeth and we shout, "Yes!" We long to love God in a way that destroys everything religious in us. We'd rather endure years of darkness and the depths of desolation if it brings us into deeper communion with God. The timing is right to move into the battle for people's souls with a vision of true goodness. The time for SoulTalk has come!

REFLECT ON A PERSONAL EXAMPLE

As you begin to *think vision*, I encourage you to reflect on one person's life who illustrates a vision of true goodness, either through written biography or personal relationship. What does spiritual formation look like, not in concept but in reality? If we can hold a clear picture in our mind of at least one person in whom Christ has been powerfully formed, we'll be strengthened to keep on *thinking vision*, to long for the spiritual journey when all we see around us—and in us—is more religion.

The Lord gave me a vivid picture of spiritual formation in my father a month before he died. I share the story to encourage you to look for similar pictures that will help you see a vision of true goodness.

We moved my aging parents closer to family when it became apparent that Dad's health was declining and Mother's Alzheimer's was advancing. Shortly after their arrival in Denver, it became necessary for Mother to receive full-time care in a facility designed for people whose minds were ravaged by that terrible disease. For the first time in more than sixty years, Mother and Dad lived separately.

They each suffered terribly, though in different ways. Mother was terrified by her confusion. Dad was devastated by the loss. So many times, I would drive home after visiting each of them in their adjoining facilities and break down. At times I screamed at God: "Is this how you treat your children? They have been your faithful servants for more than eighty years. Their last days should be spent together, enjoying each other's company until they go home. I can hardly bear their pain. Do something!"

I watched Dad visit Mother, sit next to her with his arm around her, and say, "The best is yet to come. We'll be together soon." Then Mother would be led by an attendant back to her room, behind locked doors to keep her from wandering off, and Dad would walk unsteadily back to his, with shoulders slumping, looking like the weary, worn-out old man that he was, bewildered by why he was still alive, bearing the sadness of an empty existence with no hope of things improving.

A few weeks before he died (he preceded Mother by fourteen months), I sat with him at breakfast. By this time, he was in a wheelchair, unable to walk, barely able to lift his coffee cup, unable to get a forkful of scrambled eggs to his mouth without dropping half of what was on the fork to his lap.

As I watched the life drain out of my once lively father, a strange impulse came over me that morning. I asked him a question I had never before asked, never even thought to ask in my fifty-seven years.

"Dad, have you ever had a vision?"

His eyes became instantly alert. My decidedly noncharismatic father sat up straight, filled with excitement. "I wasn't going to tell you unless you asked. Yes, I had a vision last night. It was so strange, different than anything I've ever experienced. But I don't know what it means."

"What was it?" Now I was sitting up straight.

"Well, you know how weak I've become. I need help to get out of bed and into this wheelchair. Last night, I was lying in my bed, wide awake but thoroughly tired, feeling more alone and helpless than I've ever felt, and more confused than ever by why God was allowing all this to happen, and to go on so long—Mother's Alzheimer's, my weakness. I was really depressed.

"Then I could feel myself gently being carried to a different dimension. I was still in my room, but I was in another world. The door opened—Larry, this wasn't a dream; I was wide awake; somehow this really happened—and a man came in. He was huge, muscular, and had a look of sheer evil on his face, absolutely mean. He said, 'I'm going to tear you apart. I'm going to break every bone in your body.'

"I felt terrified. I knew he could do what he said and that I was helpless to stop him. And I somehow knew God wouldn't stop him, though he could. I didn't even pray for protection. Then the man looked puzzled and said, 'I'll be back in a minute to destroy you.'

"He walked out and I just lay there, trembling. I couldn't reach the buzzer to call for help. I couldn't move. All I could do was wait. I thought of Habakkuk when he waited for the destruction he knew was coming.

"But then another thought occurred to me. He said he'd come back to destroy me. But I realized he couldn't do that. He could break my body, *but he couldn't destroy my soul.* I'm alive, and he has no power to take that away. It was the strangest thing. Lying there helpless, I felt indestructible. I *was* indestructible. That guy seemed pathetic.

"He came back in, looking mean as ever. As he walked toward me, I very calmly said, 'Look, you can do what you say. I know that and you know that. You can beat me to a pulp. But what I know and you don't know is that you can't kill or even harm my soul. I'm alive in Christ, and there's nothing you can do about that. I'm going to heaven, maybe with broken bones, but I'm going. And as soon as I get there, I'll get a new body, healthier and stronger than you'll ever be. You're a pathetic enemy. You have no real power at all.'

"The man looked at me with sheer hatred then turned to the door and left. And I lay there, more peaceful than I've felt in months. That's it. That's the vision."

I almost came out of my chair.

"Dad, I know what your vision means." I couldn't believe what I heard myself saying. I've interpreted dreams before, but never a vision. Yet I knew exactly what this vision meant.

"Dad, this world and Satan have thrown everything at you they can. You can't walk. You have next to no Christian fellowship. You've enjoyed Mom for sixty-three years, and now she doesn't even know who you are. Almost every blessing you've been given has been taken away.

"But what the Spirit has revealed in your vision is that what you want the most, you have—and no one, not even your strongest, meanest enemy, can take it away. You have God, he loves you, you're in his hands, and somehow in the middle of all this, Dad, you really are indestructible!" I was nearly shouting.

Dad listened to every word I said. His eyes danced with a life I hadn't seen for a long time. When I finished, he said, *"That's it! I'm more than a conqueror. This is wonderful."* And then he added, quietly, "I'm glad I told you my vision."

"Me too," I replied.

In that moment, my father was more completely on the spiritual journey than anyone I've known. He was delivered from religion, filled with "the love of God unto the forgetfulness of self," and yet, by losing his self he had found himself.

The experience of communion with God, of being in Christ and kept safe by the Spirit, meant more to him as we sat at breakfast that morning than any experience of blessing he could imagine. Restoring Mother's mind, enabling him to walk, giving him back the joys of fellowship in a church—nothing compared to what the Spirit revealed to him in that vision. It was all about God. First things were first.

Mother deteriorated further. Dad never walked again. He died a month later. But he had been given an experience of wholeness and life and hope and joy that not even a restored marriage could have provided. The best second things, the experience of wholeness and life and hope and joy, were granted, in the midst of ongoing sadness, because my father put first things first.

And that's the Spirit's vision, that we might value his presence above every other blessing, even when the experience of his presence is withdrawn. That's faith. And that's why Jesus died, to give us the reality of the Father's presence that we can believe in and treasure no matter what happens to us or what we feel.

AS I LOOKED AT THE HUSBAND WEEPING in my living room and at his wife sitting numb and motionless, I could *think vision.* The memory of Dad at breakfast helped. I longed for Christ to be formed in their souls until they valued fellowship with the Trinity above protection from pain, above every pleasure that second-thing blessings could provide.

The Spirit was preparing my soul to speak SoulTalk. I knew what I longed for most in both my friends' lives. I had a vision for them. I wanted them to move toward each other in a way that thrilled the Lord, in a way that would make it plain to anyone who watched that these people had been with Jesus, and that nothing mattered more. That's what it means to *think vision.* Now it's time to *think passion,* the third of our five dance lessons.

8

Look Deep into Your Own Motivation

Preparing for the Dance Lesson

Real change, the kind that transforms us into whom we most long to be and turns the world into a God-honoring community, happens when Jesus followers relate out of the deepest passion within them. Listen to astoundingly good news: *Thanks to the gospel of Jesus Christ, we have the power to change lives and transform the world.*

That power is God's pure love, not the familiar counterfeit that dresses up self-interest in lovely clothes, but the real thing: authentic, supernatural, radical, sacrificial, committed, powerful love, the energy that flows back and forth among the three persons of the Trinity and is now, because of Jesus' death, in my soul and yours.

It is our deepest passion, our strongest impulse. Because I'm a Christian, I can say that I care about you, that I want to know you, to discover who you truly are, and to help release you by touching your soul with the life of God that is in me. And I'm willing to pay a price to do that.

When I sit down to chat with you, I can realistically say, with neither hubris nor exaggeration, there is something in me that if released into you could move you toward the greatest vision anyone could have for you, whether anything in your circumstances changes or not. You can say the exact same words to me, and you'd be speaking truth. We have the power and the rhythm to dance together into the presence of God.

That's the good news. Here's the bad news: The power that's in us to change each other and the world is rarely released, and when it is, it mostly trickles out; it rarely gushes. But it could be different.

THE PASSION IS IN US

Imagine what it would be like to stir up another person's appetite for God until it became stronger than his or her appetite for answers, for control, and for every lesser blessing in life. It could happen. The passion is in us. The powerful energy to do the job is already in our soul.

Why then do we form clubs around doctrinal distinctions and call them churches? Of course we must lay theological foundations that will sometimes divide—truth matters. But why must we form an inner circle that delights to exclude others, that celebrates division so we can regard ourselves as more right than someone else and feel proud? Wouldn't it be better to stand firm on our convictions but to then speak the truth in love, to respect others without compromise, to dialogue without hypocrisy, to declare our views as we meaningfully listen to others? It won't happen as long as our passion to be right exceeds our passion to know God.

Why do we get training in relational and emotional management strategies and teach others to better control their lives, calling it therapy or pastoral leadership? Do we really love control that much? More than surrender? More than trust? More than servanthood?

And why do we support people without challenging the high value most everyone places on the good things of life? Why are we quiet when wonderful, tangible blessings are regarded as the abundant life that Jesus promised to everyone? Why do we try to use God to arrange for what we think will satisfy our soul, call our effort prayer and obedience, and then expect, with a spirit of entitlement, that good things should follow?

Our passions are too often religious and self-serving. If what we loved the most were answers that would make us think we're right about how we do church and handle life, if all we loved was control over our circumstances and relationships and personal sense of well-being, if we most loved the blessings that we define as the good life, SoulTalk could not happen. When answers, control, and blessings are in fact what we do love the most, SoulTalk cannot happen.

Back to the good news. As followers of Jesus, as children of the Father, as people with the Spirit living in our being, *we love God most deeply.* And we want to make an impact for him more than we want to make an impression for us. We want to please him more than we want to please others or win back an estranged spouse or straighten out a rebellious kid. We want to experience him more than we want to be right, to be in control, or to enjoy the good life.

Pleasing God brings pleasure into our soul.

Pleasing God brings pleasure into our soul. It's what we want to do. Pleasing others creates pressure. It's what we think we have to do. And it's tiring; it wears us out.

Because we want to, we can live to know God and find ourselves enjoying him so much we want to reveal what he's like to others. That passion is in us, and it could rule our lives. If it did, we'd speak SoulTalk. But we don't, not very often. Why?

Before we *think passion,* let's review for just a minute.

A BRIEF REVIEW

We desire to speak out of our depths into the depths of another, to speak with life-arousing power to other people. That's why I wrote this book. That's why you're reading it. We want to enter the battle for the souls of those we love.

When friends feel safe with us, they share a "journeying reality." They make known to us a little of what is really going on in their lives. They believe we care. They trust us to be curious, to actually listen, to hear without judgment, to walk with them where they are. So they take a big risk and open up.

If we're going to speak SoulTalk to them, if we're going to release the life of God out of our soul and pour it into theirs, if we're going to help people feel deeply and genuinely alive and become more like Jesus, the first thing we want to do is *think beneath*. We don't panic and run, we don't gear up to solve whatever problem they've shared, and we don't plead inadequacy as reason to immediately refer them to someone else. Instead, we listen. We wonder. We ask ourselves, What's going on in this person's soul?

Slowly, the outline of the battle between flesh (getting it right so life works) and Spirit (drawing near to God to experience his presence) begins to take shape in our minds. We see it. Because Tim can't do anything to restore his life to what it once was, he feels like quitting. He sees himself as a failure and a victim. He's despairing and bitter. Beneath his pain and fears, we can see the front-line battle. The forces of darkness value blessings; they call them life, they feel entitled to them, and they're willing to do whatever it takes to get them. If they can't, any source of numbing pleasure will do—alcohol, pornography, whatever. If they don't work, suicide seems reasonable. The forces of light want blessings, but they want God more. And God, by an act of incredible grace, is available. The battle is on. Opposing desires compete for first place.

With the battle in view, we enter it. Not by talking, but still by thinking. But now we *think vision*. Where is the Spirit taking our friend? If the battle turned in favor of the good guys, what would our friend look like? We remember that, in the gospel, our friend is fully forgiven, named as God's child and therefore welcome at the family table, stirred to want God more than any other blessing, and empowered to respond to that stirring. So we ask ourselves, What would our friend look like if his soul came alive with God's power, if his appetite for God were awakened and became more ravenous than every other desire, if he actually experienced communion with God and knew he was God's beloved, celebrated and called to a meaningful destiny? We might jot down our thoughts, even compose them into a vision letter and present it to our friend. To Tim, I could write:

> I see you continuing to hurt deeply over the many losses you've suffered that will likely never be recovered in this life. I see also a quiet strength waiting to develop in you, a centered wholeness that you will discover only as you are still before God, demanding nothing, broken by how often you've demanded so much, and repenting into abandonment to him. And I see your love for God released toward Christine with a strength she can never threaten, only rest in and enjoy, a love that will be available to all who come across your path. I see you as a secure and beloved servant who follows his Master into every storm that comes into your life. And I see you standing with him and bringing deep hope to many.

Imagine my joy as I see movement in Tim's life. I understand a little of the apostle John's heart when he spoke of his experience of communion with God and how his joy was doubled when others shared it (see I John I:I–4).

A friend shares. We *think beneath* to the real battle and we *think vision* to see what the Spirit wants to do. So what do we do? What do we say? Those questions are still premature. It's time to *think passion,* to develop a vision for ourselves as we speak, to look deep into our own motivations to see if the passion within us that is about to form words and carry them out of our mouth is religious or spiritual. Are we about to speak from holy or corrupt motives, from God-honoring or self-serving passions?

Exploring these questions, looking hard into our own interior world to see what's really going on in us as we listen to others, is how we *think passion.*

Instead of "What should I say?" here's a better question. Ask, "What's the real battle going on in my friend?" *Think beneath.* Then ask, "What do I most want to see happen in my friend's life?" *Think vision.* And now, "What stirs in me as I listen?" *Think passion.* That's our third dance lesson. We'll take it up in the next chapter.

9

Keep Looking Deep Inside

Discovering What Is Most Alive within You and Releasing It into Others

Lead with your ears, follow up with your tongue." This is good advice from James (1:19) that is nearly universally ignored. He goes on to say, "Don't be in any rush to become a teacher. . . . We get it wrong nearly every time we open our mouths" (3:1–2).

There are lots of ways we "open our mouths." Coaching, counseling, spiritual direction, therapy—we're getting confused. Culture has responded to the absence of SoulTalk by creating various approaches to guiding people through life. Coaches steer frustrated people in the workplace toward a better match of potential with opportunity. Counselors focus on personal and relational problems and do what they can to solve them. Spiritual directors remain sensitive to what God's Spirit is doing in someone's soul and flow with the process. Therapists tackle structural disorders in the personality that abuse and neglect have created and expose psychopathology in an effort to restore healthy functioning.

My vision is to see all these good things—and I believe they are good things—build on and rise from a common foundation: *the desire to see a passion for God rule in the human soul.* And I have come to believe that we can stir up that passion in each other if we discover what is most alive in us and become free enough, and authentic enough, to pour it into others.

THE "EXPERT MODEL"

The "expert model" is getting in the way of our stirring up passion in each other. Courses in coaching, programs in counseling, training in spiritual direction, and professional supervision in psychotherapy all tend to communicate, often explicitly, that effectiveness in meaningful conversation comes from what you know and how well you can apply it to someone's needs.

Society is filling up with experts, not only in medicine, plumbing, and organizational management where they rightfully belong, but also in helping people. Expertise is legitimate where highly trained people *do* something to others or to material things, like surgeons repairing bodies or electricians splicing wires; but expertise is at best questionable where change depends on real people *being* someone with another. No self-serving agendas. No points to make. No job to do. Just being, with holy passion and spiritual wisdom.

Every person who relates with people—whether as coach, counselor, spiritual director, therapist, pastor, elder, caregiver, spouse, parent, friend, or mentor—needs to speak SoulTalk. And that means we must stop talking so quickly out of what we think we know and learn to lead with our ears. If we don't, we'll be wrong nearly every time we open our mouth and, worse, we won't know it. We'll help people live the Old Way of the written code more effectively. Many will get it right and, for some of them, life will go better; but the ones for whom life does go better will have unwittingly nudged God further from the center of their lives. God will become more useful and less the point.

If we learn the discipline of silence as we engage in conversation and *think passion* as we quietly listen, perhaps we'll spend less energy figuring out what to do as experts and more energy allowing the powerful life of Christ to surface within us and be released in the words we speak. We'll leave behind the sandy foundation of expert knowledge and savvy wisdom and build instead on the solid rock of divine energy, on the foundation of life with the Trinity.

THINKING PASSION IN THREE MOVEMENTS

How can we *think passion* as we coach or counsel, or spiritually direct or therapeutically treat, or as we relate to the friends and family that we love? Our next dance lesson involves three movements.

Movement #1: *Think high enough about vision to think low enough about yourself that you're humbled into brokenness.* If our vision for others is high enough, if we actually imagine our friends wanting God more than anything else, our estimate of our own ability to make it happen will humble us profoundly. We'll see how weak and flesh-corrupted we are, and we'll despair of relating powerfully to anyone unless the life of Christ pours out of us. Brokenness, inspired by spiritual vision, is the key to releasing holy passion. Though each has its place, the key is not more training or effort.

Brokenness, inspired by spiritual vision, is the key to releasing holy passion.

Movement #2: *Reflect on your own motives as you relate.* We usually dance to Old Way music and don't know it. True brokenness comes when we see through the deception. Intentional selfishness isn't our big problem. Scores of genuinely caring people sincerely want to help others, and they want to do it in dependence on God and in line with his will. But a subtle self-centeredness can easily pollute the water from which our helping efforts flow. We can work hard to get it right so that our helping efforts succeed, and we think we are relating with spiritual energy. Brokenness that releases holy passion involves recognizing the self-deception.

Movement #3: *When you spot Old Way energy, repent.* It's all you can do. Don't try to change. Just present yourself to God as the hopeless mess you are. If he does nothing, you're sunk. When self-need rules within, when the justified demand that we get something for ourselves is our master, we speak SelfTalk. We remain committed to self-management and we depend on our resources to make things go well. But when soul-thirst, the uncorrupted counterpart of self-need, provides the energy to seek God as we talk with another, then self-management yields to soul-trust. And that happens when we identify our own self-centered motivation and fall helplessly before God. "In repentance and rest is your salvation, in quietness and trust is your strength" (Isaiah 30:15 NIV).

I long to see what is most alive in Jesus followers pour out of our souls into the people we love.

If you want to speak SoulTalk in whatever relational setting you find yourself, stay with me as we untangle these three thoughts. They're really simple. All that's needed is a willingness to honestly look at what's happening in you as you talk with others. Just lead with your ears, listen to your own inside world as well as to the inside world of others, and then follow with your tongue. *Think passion.* Let's slowly consider each of these three movements. Be patient. We'll soon be dancing.

MOVEMENT #1: EXPERIENCING BROKENNESS

Brokenness, not training or effort, is the key to discovering and releasing holy passion that makes SoulTalk possible.

As I write, I pray for a revolution in relationships. I long to see what is most alive in Jesus followers pour out of our souls into the people we love. It's happening here and there, but it needs to spread. It needs to happen all over the world. What's getting in the way? What would it take to bring in a real revolution?

The answer, I believe, is *personal revival.* Not more weeks of special meetings with dynamic speakers. Not seasons of cathartic confessions where emotions run high and repentance runs low. Not disciplined efforts to practice holy habits that we try for a while to see if they work. But real, deep, personal revival, times of refreshing that come from the Lord after dark nights of brokenness and deep repentance (see Acts 3:19).

Isaiah saw the shallow spirituality of God's people in his day and responded by crying, "Oh, that you would rend the heavens and come down, that the mountains would tremble before you!" (Isaiah 64:1 NIV). He was pleading with God to flood the earth with passionate power released through his people. One writer defined *revival* as the "reanimating of that which is already living but in a state of declension."[1]

What gets reanimated? *An appetite for God.* Listen to the psalmist: "Will you not revive us again, that your people may rejoice in you?" (Psalm 85:6 NIV). Jesus stunned his blessing-hungry audience when he said, "You're blessed when you've worked up a good appetite for God. He's food and drink in the best meal you'll ever eat" (Matthew 5:6). Revival does not provide more energy to walk the religious path, to do better so God blesses more. It rather carries us along the spiritual journey into the presence of God, where the soul's hunger is satisfied. "You will fill me with joy in your presence, with eternal pleasures at your right hand" (Psalm 16:11 NIV).

I've always been suspicious of talk about joy. Most of it

seems to encourage denial. We pretend we're not hurting. And most of what we call joy seems to depend on blessings. Get it right, and life will work. Then you can be full of joy and praise God for his goodness.

That's religion. It leads to pride or despair, never to brokenness. Religion keeps the power of God merely trickling through our lives, like water through a twisted hose. Only brokenness straightens out the kinks. Then revival comes. Living water gushes. Passion flows. What is most alive within us, a passionate desire for God himself, comes pouring out.

As Habakkuk waited for the Lord in the middle of tough times, he saw how he had not yet abandoned himself to God's vision. And then he moved from misery to joy, from discouraged confusion to released passion. "I'm turning cartwheels of joy to my Savior God," he shouted (Habakkuk 3:18).

Brokenness precedes revival. Revival reanimates the dormant life of God within us and turns it loose. Then we speak SoulTalk.

But what precedes brokenness? The answer, I believe, is an *unmanageable vision.* When we set a vision that we simply cannot achieve, we're humbled. We begin to recognize how hard we've been trying to pull off a lesser vision, to get couples communicating, to free sexual addicts, to coach corporate executives into more fulfilling opportunities. As long as we aim toward a vision we think we can reach, God lets us try. And sometimes we do pull it off. If that happens, we feel proud and call it gratitude. If it doesn't, we feel defeated and wonder why God didn't bless us.

But when we aim so high that we are forced to face how

inadequate our adequacies are, we fall flat on the ground and realize our need for spiritual power. And we admit, often for the first time, that we don't have it. Even though the church we pastor is thriving. Even though our counseling practice is booming. Even though our friends all think we're great. Even though business profits are up. There's no power coming out of us that stirs someone's appetite for God. We admit it.

Then we ask why. "God, how am I quenching your Spirit?" Then we see it. We fall on our face as we realize, "God, I've been making life work without desperate dependence on you. As long as my vision was within my reach, I've merely used you. I've not abandoned myself to you. My 'little sins' didn't get in the way of my lesser vision. But now I see that they're getting in the way of spiritual power flowing through me toward spiritual vision. And that makes these little sins big. Continuing grudges. Competition for recognition. Power plays in staff gatherings and board meetings. Weariness in well-doing that excuses laziness and justifies my insistence that others notice me. Ten-second peeks at pornography. A few minutes of 'harmless' fantasies before I go to sleep. Materialism hidden beneath gratitude to God for a good income. Resentment at my spouse for not coming through for me. A commitment never to hurt again like that. The resolve to be in control of how my kids turn out. Too much television that helps me pretend I'm not lonely."

We cry from our heart, "Lord, have mercy." No more wailing from our bed that life isn't working as it should (see Hosea 7:13–14). We enter the purifying darkness of confession and emerge into the morning light, humbled and desperately dependent.

And we wait. We stumble weakly into conversations about important matters with people we love. Our impotence to move others toward God's vision for them opens us to deep repentance. We can finally see it. We don't love our spouse like we thought. We don't care as much about the kingdom as we do about our comfort. We aren't as interested in impacting others as we are in impressing them. Our high vision has made us think low enough about ourselves that we're humbled into brokenness. And in the darkness we begin to see ourselves more clearly, to see subtle sinfulness in our motivations. That's the second movement.

MOVEMENT #2:
SEEING OUR SELF-CENTEREDNESS

True brokenness depends on seeing not only our visible selfishness, but also our disguised self-centeredness.

Visible selfishness, a clear violation of love and moral standards (like an affair), is hard to deny. Most Jesus followers agree it's bad. Yet disguised self-centeredness continues in devoted Christians unchecked and unchallenged.

I never yelled at Tim. I don't think I was ever intentionally demeaning or unkindly sarcastic. I said a few strong sentences and painted one or two hard-to-receive images, but I don't believe you could watch a video of our conversations and point to a single clear and visible act of selfishness on my part.

Satan easily seizes that fact to persuade me that my passions are holy, that my motives are good, and that my focus needs to be on helping Tim, not on seeing myself more clearly. I'm doing fine. It's Tim who needs the help. Yet I tried to impress him. That's just a little sin, a bit of neurotic insecurity, isn't it? It's not really a problem, if my vision is low.

Last night, I had dinner with a friend who talked the whole time about himself. I listened for two hours. He never asked me a question. I asked him a dozen. I left feeling rather patient and more than a little noble—*I am one good listener.*

He was visibly self-preoccupied. Watch a video of that conversation with me, and we could quickly become two head-wagging Pharisees who wonder how people can be so blind to their own self-absorption. I was the good guy, the one who led with my ears and kept my tongue still, just as James told me to do. And you'd probably agree.

I didn't see through my own deception until I began writing this chapter. I was not visibly selfish, but I was subtly self-centered. As I let him talk, I felt superior, judgmental but with a long-suffering smile.

No power came out of his soul into mine. Why? Because of his obvious self-preoccupation. No power came out of my soul into his. Why? Because of my disguised self-centeredness. Two hours of conversation and not a word of SoulTalk. Two saints unaware that they were only speaking SelfTalk. It happens all the time.

I can continue to wag my head and judge him. Or I can bow my head and judge myself. The logjam in my own eye is big.

Until tears of brokenness wash it away, I will not see his battle clearly, I will not envision the Spirit's dream for him with exciting clarity, and I will not discover enough of the grace-filled passion of Christ in me to let it flow freely out of my soul and into his.

True brokenness depends not only on seeing visible selfishness, but also on discerning the deep self-centeredness that energizes my words even as I relate with warmth and interest. And when I see it, I am in a position to experience revival, to become an unkinked hose through which the power of Christ's passion can flow. Follow me now into the third movement of *thinking passion*, which builds on the first two.

MOVEMENT #3:
RELEASING OUR HOLY PASSION

Brokenness releases the holy passion lying dormant in the depths of our soul.

The good thing about looking inside yourself is that if you stick with it, eventually you discover sunken treasure lying deep in the sea, buried but waiting for someone with the perseverance and courage to follow the Spirit and dig it up. Yet the treasure is positioned right beneath a huge iceberg—the human personality.

The ice jutting up above the waterline, what the untrained eye can easily see, represents the visible things we do, the choices we make, the emotions we feel. We brush our teeth, snip at our spouse, kiss our kids good night, worry about bills, feel irritable at work, experience mild depression when the sun goes down, enjoy a round of golf, and listen to a friend talk about himself for two hours over dinner.

Most of us deal with personal sin at this level. When we sneak a peek at *Playboy* in the convenience store or yell at our spouse or colleague or rudely tell our friend he's boring us, we know we're wrong. At least we should. And we try to deal with it. We promise God we'll never do it again, we ask a friend to hold us accountable to avoid porn, we apologize to whoever knows, whomever we hurt, and we move on—maybe with prayer and fresh resolve to read our Bibles more often and to be nicer and more holy.

That's often the extent of our brokenness. And if it is, when we speak with a friend, we may commiserate, empathize, pray, advise, explore, and care, but we don't speak SoulTalk.

So we must go deeper. Beneath the waterline is a huge mass of painful memories, arrogant demands, real or imagined threats, stubborn resolves, and firm ideas about what we want and what we hope to avoid. Drop through all of that to the bottom layer of ice and you'll find *self-need*. Let me define the term.

We were created by a relational God to enjoy relationship, first with him, then with others. We were designed to love, so we were given the capacity to receive and give the love our Creator wanted us to enjoy. When we receive love from God then give love to others, our soul is healthy. We are living according to design.

Everyone enters this world with a primary motivation to receive love and to give love in relationships, and when that happens, a deep sense of well-being develops. But there's a problem. Something's gone wrong, badly wrong, with our capacity to enjoy love.

We do not naturally trust God's love. We no longer see him as the sun around which all the planets revolve. We fail to honor God by abandoning ourselves to him with full confidence that his love will fill our soul. *We've lost our appetite for God.*

So now we're in a pickle. Because we've withdrawn from God to eat somewhere else, God has withdrawn from us. He respects our freedom to not want him. If we instead want our own way, God will let us have it. So we eat in a pigpen and think we're at a country club enjoying the richest of fare. We're served slop and enjoy it as though it were a fine dining experience. The result is that we do not experience the joy of communion with God. We no longer live with satisfied desires; we live instead with desperate needs, needs that feel justified because they're so essential to our nature. We live, not to enjoy what we've been given, but to experience what we lack. We're angry and demanding. All because we've turned away from God.

When we don't receive what we believe we need, we feel pain—deep, personal, soul-wrenching disappointment. When we do get what we're after—health, money, golf memberships, great family, applauded ministry—we still feel, in our quietest moments, an agonizing emptiness. Nothing matters more than relieving that pain and filling that emptiness. We are ruled by the consuming passion of *self-need.* To use Augustine's phrase, we are completely caved in on ourselves.

A spirit of entitlement develops. We silently communicate

to whomever is listening, "Look! I'm miserable, scared, and empty. I need to be loved. I need to feel worthwhile." But there's no one we can count on to hear and respond. Only God has the love we need, yet we've turned away from him, except to demand convenient instructions and cooperative help. So we manage every relational encounter with self-need as our ultimate value. We talk about topics we can handle. We try to build our mate's self-esteem so we can feel good about ourselves. We pout so friends will ask what's wrong. We tell jokes to keep from revealing loneliness. Self-need plus self-management, a spirit of entitlement and an attitude of independence, become the foundation of our lives, the bottom layer of ice. We become hopelessly religious.

Without Jesus, that's it. There is no sunken treasure. The iceberg rests on dirt. There is no opposing motivation beneath self-need and self-management. Religion is the bottom line.

But look deeper. By faith believe what the Bible says. Our rebellion has been forgiven, though our self-need and self-management remain. Beneath all its ugliness, however, is a restored capacity to enjoy God's love. We now have an appetite for him. We're now capable of enjoying him as our supreme prize.

Call that renewed capacity *soul-thirst*. And call our newly granted power to abandon ourselves to him *soul-trust*. Soul-thirst competes with self-need. Soul-trust opposes self-management.

Now, here's the point. The bottom layer of ice is melted only by the heat of brokenness. Nothing else is hot enough. When we see our self-centeredness and hate it, the power beneath the iceberg begins to flow into our personalities, melting the ice as it surges upward. Brokenness releases the holy passion lying dormant in the depths of our soul. And when it reaches our tongue we speak SoulTalk. We speak out of a satisfied appetite for God.

PAUSE TO ASK SOME KEY QUESTIONS

If we want to speak SoulTalk, we'll need to look deep into our motivation, to probe beneath our visible selfishness to see our invisible self-centeredness, until in brokenness and repentance we wake up to our consuming appetite for God, and the holy passion of his love burns its way into our being and is released through our words.

Do I manipulate or minister? Am I bolstering my sense of well-being when I speak with you, or am I eager to bolster yours? Do I see to it I never look bad, or do I provide the safety for someone else to look bad in the presence of grace? Is everything else, including my desire to bless you and to see you doing well, a second thing to my first-thing desire for God?

As I enter the battle for the souls of people I love, these are the questions I need to be asking. And I need to expect the answers will be disturbing and convicting. When they are, I will experience a brokenness that releases the power of God out of my life to ignite the fire in someone else's—and the revival spreads.

That's what it means to *think vision.*

10

KNOW THAT YOU HAVE SOMETHING TO SAY

Entering Another's Story with Transcendent Curiosity

O<small>K, I'VE READ NINE CHAPTERS OF YOUR BOOK</small> so far,"
you might be saying, "and I think I'm following most of what
you've been saying. I'm not dancing yet, but I think I'm getting
ready. Let me tell you what's been happening.

"A close friend of mine has been letting me in on a struggle
he's going through, and I've been *thinking beneath*. I have some idea
what the real battle is. We all try to do whatever it takes to feel
pretty good, and we think that if our lives go smoothly, we'll be
fine. And you're calling that religion.

"You're not saying there's anything wrong with wanting to
feel good, but we are wrong to look for real joy in something
other than God. And you're telling me that Christianity is
different, that it's not about being good so good things happen
to us, but it's all about knowing God no matter what happens
and enjoying him for who he is rather than trying to use him to

get whatever we think will make us happy. So the battle beneath our struggle is between trying to make life work for us and living in the New Way of the Spirit.

"I guess I can see what you mean. Jack, the friend I mentioned, is an associate pastor at the church I attend. The elders just called him in to tell him he's got a bad attitude and to warn him he might lose his job. Jack's really ticked. He sees the whole thing as a political mess. The head pastor is really insecure, a control freak who wants everyone to think he's great and to support everything he does. Jack's the one guy on staff who says what he thinks and doesn't bow and scrape to the pastor. So the pastor rats on him to the elders, and they call Jack in to tell him he has a bad attitude.

"I felt like telling Jack to just stand his ground because I think he's right, but to do it as nicely as possible. But I bit my tongue and tried to *think beneath.* I think what you'd say is that Jack's real problem is not with the pastor or the elders, even if the guy is a tyrant and the elders are a bunch of yes men. I can see now that Jack is trying to decide how to handle this thing honorably in the hope that it will all come out OK and, if that's his priority, he's turned God into a false god of convenience and cooperation.

"If Jack could hear the Spirit talking to him, he'd still be upset with the whole situation and even mad because it is unfair, but he'd be more interested in knowing God better and enjoying the Father, Son, and Holy Spirit than in straightening out his job problems. And if his appetite to experience the life of God was stronger than his desire to see his job go well, he'd probably handle the whole mess better, and his situation might improve. But even if it didn't, he'd feel peace and actually be closer to God.

"It gets a little complicated though. Jack says he wants to honor God in all this, but I hear him saying that he wants to get it right so God lets him keep his job. And I understand that. He's scared. His wife's pregnant with their third kid, and they need the money. I haven't told him that I think he's being religious, but he really is. He's trying to manipulate God. We've been meeting for breakfast, and I've been trying to *think vision* rather than telling him where I think he's off base. That's the second thing you talk about, right?

"I've been trying to picture how Jack would be looking at all this if he saw God as a Trinity of three persons having a party that he was invited to. I can't make that practical yet, but it's coming clear. At least I think I'm asking the right questions. What would he do, how would he feel, if he really knew God's life was in him, and if he wanted that more than he wanted the pastor to get fired and for the elders to offer him the job; or, than if he could keep the job he has without being hassled so much, which would be OK too?

"And I've been *thinking passion.* I've been noticing what I'm feeling as Jack and I talk about all this stuff. Listen, I can't stand the pastor. My wife and I had decided to change churches before this whole flap with Jack started. I think this guy's on a huge ego trip that keeps him from hearing the Spirit, but he always comes across like he and God are really tight. His sermons feel like a performance, and everybody leaves talking more about what a great speaker he is than about God.

"But seeing what *I'm* feeling as Jack talks has made me wonder if I'm so mad that I can't hear the Spirit either. And here I am judging the pastor for the same thing. Maybe I really like hearing bad things about the guy from Jack, and maybe my support for Jack comes out of my frustration with the pastor. To use your word, maybe all I'm doing with Jack is speaking SelfTalk.

"Maybe I shouldn't have, but I told Jack yesterday that I enjoy hearing how the pastor is messing up and that I really think that's wrong, that *I'm* wrong. It sure isn't like Jesus.

"It's really something. When I faced *my* bad attitude, I could see Jack differently. The particulars of his battle started coming into focus. I can see how he gets defensive with the elders and how he comes across as pushy and ungracious with people who get in his way. And that's Jack's battle, isn't it? If he's trying to make something happen, he'll act mad at whoever gets in his way.

"But I don't know what to do next. I've been *thinking beneath* and *thinking vision* and *thinking passion,* and now I think I'm getting in too deep. Maybe this is all leading me toward SoulTalk, but I want to walk the other way. You know, just tell Jack I'll pray for him, show some real concern when he talks about the mess at church and be as supportive as I can, and maybe give him some advice if anything occurs to me.

"That feels pretty weak to me now, but I've got to tell you, I'm feeling pretty uncomfortable. I don't know if what I'm seeing in Jack and in me is important. Maybe it's just getting too introspective. But if it is important, I don't know what to do about it. Do I just tell him what I've observed? I don't want to just rebuke him, but if I asked him what's going on, something really major might come out. Then what would I do?

"I'm not sure I want to go any further with all of this. I'm not trained for deep stuff. If I get curious about what's going on and he opens up and tells me his story, I don't know what I'll find. I sure don't want to play amateur psychologist or anything. I'm just a friend. *What's a friend supposed to do?*"

WHAT'S A FRIEND SUPPOSED TO DO?

That's a fair question. What *can* a friend do? Can this man really enter Jack's story with a curiosity that might recognize what is truly important? Can he then speak with supernatural power into whatever he finds?

It's time for the fourth lesson in SoulTalk. But first, let's quickly review the first three. Jack's friend has learned them well and repeated them pretty clearly, but to make sure we're moving to the fourth lesson without confusion over the first three, a brief summary seems in order.

So far we've been listening to someone we love telling us about a "journeying reality," about something that's come up in his life that's causing him some concern.

We've been talking to ourselves about the real battle going on beneath the journeying reality. That was the first lesson: *think beneath.* We've seen the battle between religion and Christianity, and we've discovered that it's a fierce, intense fight that's being fought in all of our souls. On the one hand, we're all trying to make life work with or without God's help. On the other, something in us wants to cling to God, to enjoy the life the Trinity enjoys, and to become more like Jesus. We want to experience the sheer thrill of relating with God and others in recklessly self-abandoning love. But we also want our lives to go well.

And we've been talking to ourselves about what is and what could be, about where the person is right now on his journey and where he could be if the Spirit has his way. That was the second lesson: *think vision.* We've realized that every time we meet someone, we're watching a terrible tragedy unfolding that is filled with brilliant hope.

Children of God—and everyone else—think nobody loves them enough for them to let go of control. It's true of Jack, the associate pastor in trouble with his elders. But *think vision!* Imagine what could be. The Son came to earth to connect us to God, to die for our sins so we could become as acceptable to the Father as he always has been.

Gently, though it doesn't always feel that way, the Spirit is detaching Jack from everything he's turned to for life, especially his own controlling style of relating. He lets Jack feel how miserable he is beneath all his posturing, how empty he feels even when the pleasures of power and safety are keeping him functioning.

And through the Spirit, Jesus is asking Jack to admit how weary and pressured and worn out he feels, how thoroughly sick he is of religion; and he's inviting him, as a deeply loved child of the Father who is full of unfelt life, to get away with him and feel that life. That's what goes through our mind when we *think vision.*

And then we've been talking to ourselves about what it would take to actually move someone toward that vision, to awaken that person's appetite for God. The question is, Do we have what it takes? If we're to do any real good, it takes the passion of Christ ruling in our soul, energizing our words, and directing our aim. So we've looked inside, and we've paid attention to what is going on inside us as we listen to someone else talk. That was the third lesson: *think passion.*

It's not been fun. We've seen anger, frustration, pride, impatience, fear, jealousy, pettiness, competition, genuine concern, empathy, a desire to help, and an excitement when we impact others that we mistake for soul satisfaction. We've seen the whole gamut of natural emotions and reactions inside ourselves, some clearly ugly, some apparently noble. And we've realized nothing we've found has any power to move anyone one inch toward our vision.

We've been tempted to lower our vision, to settle for helping someone feel better. Maybe we could help our friend handle a tough situation well or find a good match for his or her talents or experience more fully the joys of masculinity or femininity, or understand why our friend's son is so rebellious and then help the father learn to respond more effectively.

We've resisted that temptation. We've seen how incredibly wonderful the vision of the gospel really is—that we can participate in the life of God—and we want that for ourselves and for our loved ones more than we want anything else. So our vision remains supernatural.

But when we look honestly at ourselves, we feel decidedly

unsupernatural. We're helpless. We can't do miracles. We can't wash away the dirt and make ourselves clean. Even our noblest intention is stained with self-centeredness.

So we sit with someone we love, seeing the battle, seeing the vision, and seeing ourselves. And we feel broken and defeated. We can't dance. We can't even crawl. We have absolutely no power to help anyone fight his battle in a way that moves him closer to the vision. We're silenced. We're stilled. Our only hope is that God is God and that he is here. Brokenness lets us see our impotence enough to repent of self-sufficiency. Then we abandon ourselves to God. He really is our only hope.

Internally, as we listen to our friend talk, we're crying out. Out of the depths of despair we cry to the Lord. We cry for mercy. We deserve nothing. Our confidence is in God's kindness, nothing else, certainly not in ourselves. And we wait. Our soul waits for the Lord, and in his Word we put our hope (see Psalm 130:6). To wait for God means to wrap ourselves around him. It isn't a passive thing. We confess our unworthiness, our inadequacy, our self-centeredness, our lack of trust, our fallenness. But we keep going to him.

We beg God to speak out of our depths into another's soul, to awaken that person's appetite for Christ. We know what we most long to see take place in our friend, but we have no power in ourselves to make it happen. And then something happens. We experience the *joy* of dependence, the *thrill* of needing God. Abandonment to God releases confidence in him. We realize we're already possessed by him. We are participants in his life.

We're not unworthy. We're Christians. The Spirit lives in us. The life of God is at our core, waiting to spill over into someone else.

And we relax. The pressure's off. We confidently and humbly declare our availability to God. We move from brokenness to power; we feel ourselves becoming centered in Christ, no longer in ourselves. We're quiet. We notice we're not scrambling anymore. We're not nervously compelled to speak. If we say nothing that makes a visible impact, we're OK with that. We're comfortable with saying nothing. It is then that we begin to believe that we really do have something to say. Confidence in the Father's availability, in the way to the Father opened up by the Son, and in the Spirit's presence becomes real, central, and invigorating.

The life of God is at our core, waiting to spill over into someone else.

We know we can enter the battle for another's soul with the energy of Christ. We believe the passion of Christ is supplied by the Spirit and directed to the Father and that it could pour out of our soul into another's and actually awaken the hibernating life of God that lies dormant in that other person's depths. It might take time, perhaps years. But we're in no rush. Our first-thing desire is to participate in God's life and release it from our depths in any way that suits the need of the moment. What happens is always a second thing. And that's what it means to *think passion*.

READY FOR THE NEXT STEP

Now we're ready. So far we've been talking to ourselves, *thinking beneath* to see the battle, *thinking vision* to see what the Spirit longs to do, and *thinking passion* until we're humbled into dependence on the Spirit for anything good to happen. Now it's time to say something, to walk confidently onto the dance floor and begin to move in rhythm with the Spirit.

We know we have something to say, but what is it? What words will take us into battle, aim toward God's vision, and carry the Spirit's power into someone's soul? What can we say that will wake someone up to his or her desire for God?

Please consider one idea that I believe to be terrifically important but commonly overlooked: *People will not move as far as they could on their journey into God's presence or experience the power of the Spirit as fully as they could without telling their story to another person.*

No lie is more often believed than the lie that we can know God without someone else knowing us. Keeping secrets is lethal. The core of individualism is pride, and pride isolates. We can keep our sexual desires in check and we can stop drinking too much and we can give ourselves to our mate in loving servanthood and we can parent our kids with diligence and we can recognize our demand to be in control—all without ever drawing close enough to another person to have him or her see us as we really are.

But deep change requires community, and community is always mutual. We must be willing to tell our story if we expect others to tell us theirs.

Let's *think story*. That's our fourth dance lesson. We need to learn one movement. I call it *transcendent curiosity*.

We must lead with our ears into the particular story of someone's life. Curiosity begins the process. But not empathic curiosity. Our purpose is not merely to hear what another is feeling. We want to discern what the forces of darkness have been deceitfully saying to our friend; we want to recognize the Spirit's whispers of truth coming from deep places in our friend's soul that may yet be unheard. That's *transcendent curiosity*.

Read the preceding paragraph again. It's important. It's so important that I devote the entire next chapter to discussing transcendent curiosity. If we know what it means and learn to be transcendently curious, we'll be off to a good start in thinking story.

11

LISTEN TO MORE THAN THE STORY YOU'RE TOLD

Moving Beyond Empathy and Accountability to Transcendent Curiosity

WHAT DOES IT MEAN TO LISTEN, really listen, when someone shares a problem? How do we enter the battle in a loved one's soul when she makes known a concern, or when it's evident she's troubled by something? What mistakes do we need to avoid? Now that we're ready to talk, not just to ourselves in internal dialogue as we *think beneath, think vision,* and *think passion,* but to others in spoken conversation, what do we say?

It's time to *think story.* How do we verbally engage with a friend as she lets us in on her struggles? How do we "get beneath" to her particular battle? This is the fourth lesson in SoulTalk.

TRANSCENDENT CURIOSITY

The dance step we're about to learn is easily described: Move beyond empathy and accountability to the most unpracticed relational movement in modern culture—*transcendent curiosity.* It may be easily described, but it's rarely seen in actual conversation.

We so effortlessly and so mindlessly say, "Sounds like you feel . . ." or, "I really think you should . . ." It's so unnatural to say, "I think I see the outline of a fierce battle going on within you. Think about it with me. What happens in you when . . ."

SoulTalk does not specialize in empathy or focus on accountability. SoulTalk, the language of the Spirit that arouses another's appetite for Christ, evidences gentle but relentless curiosity about the battle between despair and hope, control and freedom, indifference and love, about the cosmic war that is going on every minute in the depths of the human soul.

When a woman tells the story of her rape, if we're not stirred to our bones with trembling compassion, we'll never speak SoulTalk. If we're detached in any measure from her soul-wrenching pain, the broken heart of Jesus will never be experienced through us. We'll never dance together with her into the presence of God.

But if we hear *only* her pain, if we're caught up with no greater longing than wanting to see her reclaim the dignity of her womanhood and to recover the enjoyment of her miraculously unmarred beauty, we'll never move beyond SelfTalk.

And that's what we tend to do. It's how we think. We've shrunk the gospel down to the promise of recovery. Recovery from abuse. Recovery from divorce. Recovery from loneliness after a spouse's death. Recovery from addiction. Recovery from self-hatred, worry, and depression. Recovery from whatever wounds we've suffered, whatever trauma we've endured, whatever pain or emptiness we feel.

The modern gospel promises recovery from anything that keeps us from feeling alive and whole and free. Jesus, we think, came to give us the abundant life of less pain and more pleasure, less boredom and more adventure, less fear and more confidence, less conflict and more harmony. And, by golly, we're going to get all that's coming to us. That's how many Christians think.

SUBSTITUTING RELIGION
FOR CHRISTIANITY

A switch has been made, a subtle one but real. The point now is how I feel about me. The person who can provide me with the experience I want is Jesus. So I follow him for the same reason I frequent my favorite restaurant: They both give me what I want. I love Jesus the same way I love the restaurant.

Make no mistake: Jesus *did* come to give us life. He is the only good meal in town. He saw that we were empty, hungry, weary, and burnt out on religion, and he told us to get away with him. And the incentive was clear: "Get away with me and you'll recover your life" (Matthew 11:28). Certainly that means we'll feel alive, that our experience will include a sense of purpose and freedom and adventure and hope. He will feed our soul. Our hunger will be satisfied, with him.

But notice: *Jesus did not tell us to recover our life.* He did not tell us to restore our soul. He told us to get away with him. His death and resurrection opened the path for us to draw near to God (see Hebrews 7:18). *That's* what we're to be about. That's what we're to do as the focus of our life. And we're to do it for his glory, which wonderfully includes our well-being. But our well-being isn't the point! It's not incidental, of course. God is thrilled that we come alive. But his being thrilled is the point.

We've turned the incentive into the goal. We've switched first and second things. Our focus now is on coming alive. Drawing near to God, getting away with Jesus, keeping in step with the Spirit have become useful things to do, useful to us. Fellowship with God has become self-serving; worship is one more expression of narcissism.

I was with Brennan Manning just before he went on a silent retreat for seven days. With unrecognized pragmatism, I asked what these retreats did for him. He looked a bit puzzled, then said, "I guess I've never thought about what they do for me. I just figure God likes it when I show up." Brennan was far more concerned with God's pleasure than his own—which, of course, guaranteed Brennan's pleasure. He hadn't made the disastrous switch.

But most of us have. The end we're after is not relationship with God; it's the usefulness of relationship with God. We want to feel a certain way, experience life a certain way, enjoy the internal reality we most want to enjoy.

In our culture, and especially in postmodern spirituality, the gospel has been reduced to a "much better plan" for experiencing good feelings about our life that every self-aware soul longs to feel. We yearn to experience a life of adventure and freedom and passion and beauty and meaning and intimacy and value. And in words that sound so Christian, we declare it's all available, but only in Christ.

We don't see that we've substituted religion for Christianity. We've given up on money and fame and success as the route to fulfillment. Now it's Christ. Through him we can be free. But it's still religion. We get it right so our life works.

Our version of the good news no longer showcases Jesus as the way to recover and enjoy relationship with God.

The switch has been made. Our enjoyment of the life we've always wanted has become the priority. God's pleasure is not even taken into account. And the sheer rightness of living for God is marginally relevant at best. We're still the focus. God has become our tool, the preferred means to our narcissistic goal—which opens the possibility that if, at some point, we judge that he is not producing, we might choose a different path.

Our version of the good news no longer showcases Jesus as the way to recover and enjoy relationship with God. We don't see Jesus as our ticket into the party where the Trinity is dancing. He's now the means to something less, which we regard as more.

Jesus has been downgraded to the Great Therapist who helps us recover ourselves. We go on a treasure hunt, looking for ourselves, and Jesus provides the map and the energy to follow it. We no longer value his power to awaken and satisfy our appetite for God. The desire to find ourselves is stronger. Intimacy with God, even though it restores the enjoyment of our beauty and value and introduces us to who we really are, is no longer our highest vision.

Instead, we turn to Jesus for what we need to become happily intimate with ourselves. We want to like who we are in spite of neglect and rejection, to live with a warm appreciation for our unique identity no matter who devalues us, to enjoy relating with people who affirm our worth and treat us with respect and respond to our low times with loving sensitivity.

As we now understand the gospel, it frees us to dance to heavenly music in a way that lets us love, not lose, our life on earth. And then we look for others who appreciate the same music, with whom we can kick it up together, and we start our own party. That's our version of community. If we find enough people, we call it church.

Once a week, we stop dancing long enough to tip our hat to Jesus for renting the hall, to the Father for happily watching us tear it up, and to the Spirit for playing the music we like. And we call it worship.

THE INADEQUACY OF EMPATHY

When sanctification was wrongly defined as rule keeping, admonition and accountability were the basic tools of the trade. Now that recovery is mistaken for sanctification, empathy has replaced admonition as the method of choice, as the center of SoulCare—which is like getting over the shingles and contracting tuberculosis.

If we're thinking recovery, when a loved one shares a struggle we tend not to *think advice*, but instead to *think empathy*. We're less likely to quickly say, "Well, I think you need more time in the Word" or, "Maybe you're depressed because you're feeling sorry for yourself. You need to get more involved at church. Are you in a Bible study?"

Now that gospel living has traded an emphasis on conformity to standards for recovery from pain, we've become more empathic when people share their struggles. We're inclined to remain warmly and thoughtfully quiet for a moment, then say, "I can't imagine what you're feeling. I will pray faithfully for you" or, "What you're going through must feel like it's killing your soul. You must be so angry that you've never been loved well."

Then what? Some of us still fall back on advice. Enlightened moderns often *think healing*. We think in the imagery of wounds and healing more than of disease and cure or sin and rebuke. Healing prayer, healing the memories—we're looking for some ritual, some retreat, some method of prayer or practice of spiritual disciplines that will recover our joy, or some new approach to community where we can discover our freedom and come alive.

If we're not trained in healing methods, or if we're reluctant to try new styles of community, we *think support*. Perhaps this is what's most common in both religious and secular culture. Support groups. Supportive counseling. Friends who offer support. "I hear what you're going through. It sounds awful. I want to pray for you and stand by you and walk with you for as long as it takes."

As long as it takes *for what?* To feel better, of course. To get away from the source of pain. To find a way to manage life that doesn't hurt as much.

When someone is seeking the Lord and we offer nothing but empathic support, we're putting band-aids on infected wounds; we're passing out aspirin to cancer patients.

No, it's worse than that. When empathy is our primary response to pain, we strengthen narcissism, which is a fancy word for depraved self-centeredness. And the Father and the Son and the Spirit and the community around us are all expected to cooperate in helping us honor our self-focused agenda. The flesh still rules. We're still caved in on ourselves.

When someone we love shares a burden, to not hear her pain is inhuman. To not feel it and not let her know we feel it is ungodly. To not resonate with deep human desire and hurt when it's disappointed is wrong. We are to weep with those who weep. We rightly long for dead people to wake up, for wounded people to be healed, and for hurting people to feel better.

But to see nothing more destructive to the human soul lying beneath pain is cruel, and to see no greater good than relief from pain is diabolical. It's a response from hell. It keeps us preoccupied with ourselves and no closer to God.

Before the therapeutic revolution and the advent of post-modernism, we thought the bottom line in SoulCare was spot-

ting sin and confronting it. Years ago, a veteran biblical counselor instructed me that good counseling consisted of listening
to people tell their stories until I heard a violation of biblical
principles. Then I was to pounce. Admonish. Rebuke. Exhort.
Correct. Teach.

Now that the bottom line has shifted away from moral
commanding to empathic relating, to seeing the world through
another's eyes and feeling what they feel as they encounter life,
we've largely given up trying to get people to simply apply
biblical principles to their lives. Now we want to find a way to
heal their wounds, to release their freedom. Christians used to
promote conformity. Now we provide healing experiences—
neither is SoulTalk.

Should we then not talk to people about their responsibility
to obey biblical principles in their specific situation? Is feeling
people's pain and wanting to heal the wounds that cause the
pain a bad thing? Can't we do both, first empathize then guide
or exhort? What exactly are we to do? What does it mean to be
transcendently curious as we listen to someone tell us her story?

RESPONDING TO A FRIEND

Your friend shares that she was raped years ago. Now she is
married to a man whose level of insensitivity can only be
described as cruel. He wants sex whenever he wants it, with no
thought whatsoever of the impact her hideous memories have
on this most delicate and vulnerable act. He never embraces her
with tenderness. Every physical touch is foreplay, a prelude to

what he's after. He never cherishes his wife by sacrificially responding to what she wants. He simply doesn't care.

As she tells you her story, your heart nearly bursts with compassion for her and rage toward her husband. You realize that not a day goes by when her wound is not reopened by this awful man. And then with reliable and meanspirited indifference to what she is feeling, he pours salt into her wound and rubs it in with grimy hands.

You can't even think of holding her accountable in the middle of her agony, at least not right away. To discuss the meaning of submission after she's just opened her heart would be pouring more salt into her wound. You feel her pain deeply. You hurt for her. Your eyes brim with tears. You long to be with her, to be present to her as a caring, supportive friend. You want her to recover her life as a valued and cherished and beautiful woman. To desire less would poorly reflect Christ. But what do you do?

Remember the first three dance lessons. *Think beneath.* Ask yourself, What is the most significant battle she is facing right now? Realize that she is feeling the demand to protect her soul from further pain, and that demand seems eminently reasonable. What higher priority could there be? But that's the Old Way—do something to make your life work.

Think, too, about the Spirit within her, gently urging her to abandon herself fully to God, to value intimacy with him over every other good, to make herself available to God's purposes, to yield herself to the process of becoming more like Christ, and to trust the Spirit for godly passion and spiritual wisdom as she responds to her husband. That's the New Way—draw near to God as your better hope. And when you see the New Way, then you will see the real battle between the Old Way and the New Way. Start there in your thinking.

Then *think vision.* How would she be different if Christ were more fully formed in her? What beauty remains hidden in her soul that the Spirit longs to release as she draws near to God and values him above every other good? What would it mean for her to actually enjoy the Father and the Son and the Spirit, each one uniquely, as she responds to her terrible husband? What is the Spirit up to in her life that at first glance she might not find appealing at all, but that you would envision as a wonderful thing despite her angry protests?

Then *think passion.* Perhaps her pain resonates with the pain you've experienced in your life, maybe in your marriage. As you look into yourself, you realize how justified *you* feel in placing top priority on relieving her pain, on helping her come alive as a woman, how natural it is for you to slide into Old Way thinking. But that realization disturbs you. You know you're reflecting your bitter soul more than your loving God. So in brokenness and repentance you surrender afresh to him and begin to feel the energy of Christ rise up within you. You want to follow his Spirit into battle for this woman's soul. You want to see Christ formed in her soul. Nothing matters more.

Now you can speak with your beginning awareness of the real battle, your developing vision for the Spirit's work, and your emerging passion to arouse her appetite for God. You know you have something to say. But what is it? Do you offer empathic support? Do you suggest a biblical way of thinking and behaving? Do you probe more deeply? For what? Maybe it's best to call in your pastor, who knows God better, or refer her to a counselor who knows how to probe and what to look for.

PREPARING TO SPEAK WITH TRANSCENDENT CURIOSITY

As you prepare to speak, to engage your friend, to dance with her into the New Way to live, consider these four thoughts.

First, if you do not weep over her pain, perhaps literally, you will never speak SoulTalk. Passing quickly by her pain or minimizing it in any way will break whatever connection you may have with her. Any bridge that reaches from your soul to hers will collapse if you are not moved, as Jesus is, by her pain.

Second, if you hear nothing more than her pain, if you can envision no greater good than relief, you will speak only SelfTalk. Nothing you say will be carried by your priority desire to arouse her longing for God, to see her enjoy relating to him as her highest treasure.

Third, if you shift back from a focus on her suffering to a harsh focus on her responsibility, you run the risk of losing her. And you should. You would then be speaking traditionally religious SelfTalk, the language of legalism disguised as the language of obedience. You would be on your way to becoming like the Pharisees, those rule-imposing religious leaders most witheringly denounced by our Lord. You would speak another form of SelfTalk.

Fourth, if you moved toward her with transcendent curiosity, if you lifted your ear to hear the melody from heaven that invites her to trust the Father who watched his Son suffer so that he could welcome her to his party, then, and not until then, you would know what to say. You would be leading with your ear and getting ready to follow up with your tongue. You would sense the Spirit's rhythm in exposing hell's deception and in recognizing heaven's music. And you would speak SoulTalk.

The fourth thought is what I believe James had in mind when he told us, "Lead with your ears, follow up with your tongue, and let anger straggle along in the rear. God's righteousness doesn't grow from human anger" (James 1:19–20). "Lead with your ears" clearly means that we should listen. To what?

I think we seriously misunderstand James's intent. Modern Christians assume he wants us to be good listeners to people, not to speak too much or too quickly, but rather to hear what people are really saying. In other words, to be empathic.

But two observations make me believe that James is calling us to become transcendently curious, something entirely different from empathy. Empathy is listening to hear what someone is feeling, to identify emotions and attitudes that people might not admit or even know they are feeling or thinking.

"You sound angry as you talk about your boss."

"I wasn't aware of that, but now that you mention it, I can feel it."

That's empathy, a simplistic example perhaps, but one that quickly illustrates its core.

Transcendent curiosity is different. It involves a sense of wonder, a profound intrigue and fascination with the eternal drama that is being played out in someone's life. The first observation that persuades me that James wants us to be transcendently curious rather than empathic is what precedes his instruction to lead with our ears:

> Prosperity is as short-lived as a wildflower, so don't ever count on it. . . . At the very moment everyone is looking on in admiration, it fades away to nothing.
>
> Anyone who meets a testing challenge head-on and manages to stick it out is mighty fortunate. For such persons loyally in love with God, the reward is life and more life.
>
> Don't let anyone under pressure to give in to evil say, 'God is trying to trip me up.'. . . The temptation to give in to evil comes from us and only us. We have no one to blame but the leering, seducing flare-up of our own lust. . . .
>
> So, my very dear friends, don't get thrown off course. Every desirable and beneficial gift comes out of heaven. The gifts are rivers of light cascading down from the Father of Light. . . .
>
> Post this at all the intersections, dear friends: Lead with your ears, follow up with your tongue. (James 1:10–19)

From the context, I hear the writer saying this: Life sometimes goes great for a while. But troubles always come. And when they do, you'll feel an urge to do whatever you can to restore the good times, to relieve your pain, and in the process, to stop moving toward God with regard for him as your ultimate treasure. You must recognize that urge as coming from dark places, from your devil-inspired, world-encouraged fleshly demands. But pay close attention also to the promptings from heaven. The music is playing. You'll see the light of God's life flowing through your soul like a river. Listen for the sounds of hell's noise and heaven's music. Lead with your ears. Ask questions. Be curious. And when you can discern the difference between the sound of heaven and the sound of hell in this person's story, then speak. But not in anger.

Right now, as the woman who was raped is telling her story, deceitful desires are pressing on her from within. Listen to them: "Minimize pain. Whatever it takes, do it. Get back to whatever good life is available to you. You want to feel like a beautiful, cherished woman. Pursue that desire any way you can. If that's through Jesus, fine. If he doesn't come through, I have other suggestions."

But spiritual nudging is also gently directing her toward a different path: "God knows what he's doing. Abandon yourself to him. Notice how much you want to know him. The Father welcomes you to his party. The Son can use everything that happens to make you more like him. And the Spirit will lead you into the likeness of Christ and toward the Father's home."

When a friend tells her story, we must tune our ears to hear the screechings of hell, to recognize the ugly demand for getting one's own way so that good feelings come, and to hear the music of heaven, to that gentle but firm call to pursue the better hope of intimacy with God over every lesser hope. That's what it means to be transcendently curious.

JESUS' EXAMPLE OF
TRANSCENDENT CURIOSITY

When I read the admonition from James to lead with our ears, I wonder if Jesus serves as a model for what James wants us to do.

Read through the Gospels. Look at each recorded conversation between Jesus and someone else to see how he spoke. If James intended that we be empathic, then Jesus could not be a worse model. Not once do I find him saying, "Tell me how you feel" or, "It sounds like you're really anxious right now." If empathy is right, Jesus is wrong.

Just before his arrest, Jesus told his disciples they would blame him for their world falling apart. "Peter blurted out, 'Even if everyone else is ashamed of you when things fall to pieces, I won't be.' Jesus said, 'Don't be so sure. Today, this very night in fact, before the rooster crows twice, you will deny me three times.'"

Jesus could have said, "Peter, you're feeling a great deal of passion right now. Let's explore to see how deep it really is." That would have been at least mildly empathic (see Mark 14:27–30).

A second example involves Peter again. After Jesus had offended the Pharisees by telling them that rule keeping never made anyone holy and that wickedness comes out of the heart, Peter was confused. He wasn't sure what Jesus meant.

"I don't get it. Put it in plain language," Peter said.

"Jesus replied, 'You too? Are you being willfully stupid?'" (see Matthew 15:1–16, especially verses 12–16).

If Jesus came to me for supervision on how to relate, I might have suggested he say, "Peter, you seem eager to know what I mean. I affirm your desire to understand my teaching. Tell me what you're hearing." That would have been more gently empathic.

Instead, Jesus was tuned in to Peter's earthbound, world-confirming, flesh-driven way of thinking. I hear him telling Peter to stop jerking to the devil's noise and to start dancing to the Father's music.

One more. When Lazarus died, Mary chided Jesus for not responding more quickly to their summons. "Master, if only you had been there, my brother would not have died" (John 11:32).

What should a nondefensive, centered, compassionate man say in response? Perhaps something like, "You are deeply sad. And you are disap-pointed in me. Tell me all that you feel."

But Jesus refused the empathic way. "When Jesus saw her sobbing . . . a deep anger welled up within him. He said, 'Where did you put him?'" (vv. 33–34). Then he went off and called Lazarus out of the grave.

Whenever people spoke, Jesus looked to see which kingdom was being advanced in that moment.

Here's what I see consistently in Jesus' conversations. His focus was on discerning movement from the kingdom of hell and from the kingdom of heaven. Whenever people spoke, Jesus looked to see which kingdom was being advanced in that moment. He spoke against the devil's influence, exposing it in people's words and actions; and he spoke for his Father's agenda, calling others to abandon themselves to the kingdom of heaven, to become aware that the kingdom was present and that they could live as citizens of that kingdom.

When two blind men cried out, "Mercy, Son of David! Mercy on us!" Jesus kept walking. He didn't stop and say, "Tell me what it's been like to have been blind all these years." Instead, when they followed him home, still crying out for mercy, Jesus said, "Do you really believe I can do this?" When they answered yes, he said, "Become what you believe." He touched their eyes, and they could see (see Matthew 9:27–29).

These blind men saw the light of heaven with the eyes of their souls. When they confessed their faith, Jesus gave another sign that the kingdom was indeed present. I see little of a warm empathic conversation followed by an even warmer act of healing. I see the Messiah advancing his kingdom.

Jesus led with his ears. When he discerned movement toward God, he followed up with words of life. When he heard the influence of fleshly thinking, he spoke clearly against it. I see him as the perfect model of transcendent curiosity.

If we're going to speak SoulTalk as we listen to someone's story, if we're going to move beyond empathy and accountability to engage another with transcendent curiosity, we need to know what it would mean for us to imitate Jesus as we talk with people we love. The challenge is great. We'll take it up in the next chapter.

12
REACH INTO THE SOUL
THROUGH A PERSON'S STORY

Seizing the Opportunity for SoulTalk

WE REALLY DON'T KNOW EACH OTHER VERY WELL. So many of our stories are never told. So many of our secrets are never shared. So many of our struggles are never heard.

And that's how it should be, in most conversations. Nothing destroys community more effectively than an intimacy addict trying to turn every encounter into a soul-to-soul conversation. Give me mindless fun any day over contrived SoulTalk, which isn't SoulTalk at all.

The point is important. Every conversation can be (and should be) consistent with SoulTalk. The energy of love should permeate every relational encounter. But not every conversation can (or should) center on soul-penetrating exchanges.

A woman I once knew would reliably bring her face within six inches of mine and ask, "How *are* you? Really!" I might have just told a joke or mentioned that my wife and I were speaking at a marriage conference in two weeks. She seemed incapable of simply chuckling or saying, "Sounds great!"

It's OK to just catch up on each other's life. "How're things goin'?" "When's your son coming home from college? How's he doing?" "First trip to Hawaii? What'd you think?"

A casually empathic response—"Hey, that's wonderful!" or, "I'm so sorry to hear that"—is perfectly appropriate. Take it no further. It's OK.

And it's OK to focus on fun. Throw a Super Bowl party. And don't begin with prayer. Or if you do, simply thank God for good times—after all, he thought them up—then break out the chips, grill the burgers, and tell every dumb joke you can remember. And maybe watch the game.

Not all good conversations involve transcendent curiosity about someone's inner life. Bible studies, book clubs, dinner parties, and committee meetings each have their place. They each serve a legitimate purpose. Let your conversation honor that place and reflect that purpose.

At your Bible study, talk about Galatians, not each other's life. Discuss John Grisham's latest novel when your book club meets. Tell stories about where you've been and what you've been doing while you're enjoying a great meal. And at your committee meetings, don't zero in on how the people in the room are doing spiritually. Do what you came to do.

But if the story of your soul is *never* told, if the secrets of your heart are *never* shared, if the struggles in your life are *never* heard, then you are living the tragedy of an unobserved life. You are enduring the unnecessary anguish of loneliness.

Hear a caution. You must *not* make it your goal to tell your story, share your secrets, and make known your struggles to a listening ear. That's *not* the narrow path to joy. Rather, determine to lead with your ears so that others will tell you their stories, share their secrets with you, and make known their struggles to your listening ears.

That's what we're called to do. Yet every calling has its price. Good listeners are lonely. They long to be listened to in the same way they listen to others. As you learn the dance of SoulTalk, let me offer two thoughts about what you'll feel.

First, the loneliness you will experience as you enter the battle for another's soul will at times seem unendurable. You will hurt, you will feel resentful, you will feel smug. Let the struggles that are created by providing SoulTalk to others drive you to long nights of wrestling with God, pouring out your heart to him, wondering where he is, feeling the despairing and angry urge to give up being there for others and to live instead for yourself. Expect to feel like quitting, to experience a nearly consuming desire to find relief in things like food or pornography, or worse. And then consider the options. You'll discover a desire to know God that will keep you going on the good path, even when you slip.

Second, recognize that always being there for others is often a defense. Like me and everyone else, you're terrified to be known. It's more blessed to give than to receive, but it's also safer. So abandon your demand to feel safe and make yourself available to be heard by another. Risk sharing your secrets with one friend. Risk telling your story and making known your struggles to a small group. It will backfire at times, and you will have tales of verbal abuse to match other folks who have taken similar risks. But stay with it. To give up on soul-meeting community is to give up on life. You must not let one bite, or many bites, of poisoned food persuade you never to eat again.

SEIZE OPPORTUNITIES FOR SOULTALK

In a healthy world, most of our conversations would not involve SoulTalk, but every person would be eager to engage in SoulTalk when the opportunity arises.

Most opportunities for SoulTalk are easier to recognize than to seize. Over lunch, on the golf course, in a small group, someone will open the door to his or her life, usually just a crack.

"I've really been tired lately."

"Things aren't so good at home, but we'll manage."

"Sherry makes me so mad. Everybody caters to her."

What do you do? Ask a follow-up question? Commiserate and move on? Tell a story of your own about Sherry?

Let me share a vital but almost universally ignored principle, stated in two parts. Read it several times:

If, as a general mind-set in all your conversations, you're not already *thinking beneath, thinking vision,* and *thinking passion,* you will not know when or how to seize the opportunity for SoulTalk. You will quench the Spirit and not recognize his prompts.

If, as a general mind-set in all your conversations, you are already *thinking beneath, thinking vision,* and *thinking passion,* you will hear the music of heaven, know the movement of the Spirit, and sense a loving urge to enter someone's life through the door he or she has opened; and you will begin the dance. You will feel transcendently curious and therefore, without strategy or effort, you will invite stories, secrets, and struggles. You will *think story.*

Let me explain.

Suppose you're spending an evening with a group of close friends. Suppose further that you meet regularly with these friends for the agreed-upon purpose of walking together on your spiritual journeys.

In that setting, most Christians naturally *think empathy* rather than *thinking beneath. We think solutions* rather than *thinking vision.* And we *think help* rather than *thinking passion.* We're a community of well-meaning fixers. We therefore lead more with our mouth than with our ears. We never get around to *thinking story.* We're too busy fixing whatever we see, with little or no awareness of the ugliness staining our attitudes and our real impact on others.

A recently divorced woman told her small group, "I'm really lonely." The chorus of helpful responses was deafening. "We could sure use another worker in the children's ministry at church. You might make some friends." "Oh, Sandy, maybe you just need to hear how God right now is delighting in you. Here, let me read Zephaniah 3:17—God sings over you with delight." "You seem to stay to yourself pretty much. I don't mean to sound harsh, but I wonder if you're sliding into self-pity."

No one entered Sandy's soul through her story. No one asked a question, not even one so simple as, "I'd love to hear

you talk about that. Would you?" No one was *thinking story*.
They were too occupied with empathy, solutions, and their
desire to help. And Sandy left that evening feeling more lonely
than when she came and a little angry. Everyone else left feeling
good about his or her input.

Imagine what could happen if the people in that group were
thinking beneath. Imagine what might happen if the group
members were listening to Sandy with the category of central
battle in their minds.

"So Sandy's lonely. Hmm. I'm happily married, so I don't feel
her kind of loneliness. But our central battle is the same. If I got
far enough beneath Sandy's problems and mine, I'd see the war
we're both fighting. Every one of us is determined to make this
life work to our satisfaction. We're all addicted to feeling good,
and we've learned that something could do the job, so that's what
we're living for, whatever it is. We're really obsessed with ourselves, not with God but with using God to get our lives going
well enough so that we're happy, rather than trusting God with
our eventual well-being. I wonder what this battle looks like in
Sandy's life, beneath her feelings of loneliness."

And suppose all of them were *thinking vision*. If they were,
you'd hear something like this going on in their minds: "The
Spirit of Christ lives in Sandy. I wonder where he's taking her.
He knows right where she is—maybe she's full of self-pity,
maybe she's having an affair, but he loves her and is nudging her
toward . . . what? Sandy is so shy. She barely talks, and never with
confidence. If she were absorbed with Christ, I wonder if she'd
feel a different kind of confidence—a quiet, holy confidence

that would free her to speak from the center of her being, where she's already whole. I wonder if she ever dreams of what she could be, even in the middle of her loneliness as a divorcée."

Now suppose everyone in the group was *thinking passion*. Then the group members would be talking to themselves something like this: "I have such a long way to go. I'm feeling so irritated with Sandy. I'm really judging her. Yes, she's alone, but she's wealthy. I'd guess her settlement was pretty darn good. Look at the car she just bought. My husband just lost his job, and he's been miserable to live with. I think I'd rather be in her shoes. Boy, as long as I think like that, nothing I say will come from the Spirit. Oh, God, forgive me. I long to love Sandy, not be jealous of her."

Can you see it? If you're already *thinking beneath, thinking vision,* and *thinking passion,* transcendent curiosity will flow out of your engaged and hopeful but humble and contrite heart. You'll *think story,* and you'll gently seize the opportunity for SoulTalk.

SOULTALK IN ACTION

Here's how it happened last night with a group of friends with whom my wife and I regularly meet (with changes in the names and identifying details).

We met at five o'clock in the afternoon. Dinner was planned for seven-thirty. Our only agenda for the first two and a half hours was to enjoy each other and walk together on the journey into God's presence.

I was in a bad mood. I was just getting over a severe headache that had permitted me only two hours of sleep the night before and had kept me, once again, from making progress in writing this book. When I get in a bad mood, I become cynical and maybe more truthful.

Bill opened the evening by giving us each a copy of a book he and Lisa had just read. "This is the best book I've read in months. I'd love for us all to read it and maybe discuss it at some further date."

For half an hour, we asked Bill and Lisa to tell us what the book had meant to them. Good conversation followed. We all felt appreciative for the gift. We were drawn to the impact it had had on our friends, and we all felt quite willing to read it and to discuss it together later.

I tend to lead the group, so when that topic reached a natural completion, Bill turned to me and, with a warm smile, said, "So where do we go now?"

Normally, we begin with *lectio divina,* a special way of opening our ears to the Spirit as we read a biblical text. Then someone invites the group to join him on his spiritual journey as he makes known where he is. Last night I skipped *lectio* and moved right away to where I was.

"Well, I've had one of my miserable headaches for the last day. It still hurts but not as bad. When I go through this, I lose perspective. Right now I'm wondering what exactly is the point of prayer, at least for physical things. I don't think I've ever seen someone recover from a medical problem in a way that could only be explained as an answer to prayer.

"Even my cancer. Yes, I'm glad you all prayed. I'm healthy

now. And if it comes back, I want you to pray again. But I think I'm healthy because I had a good surgeon. Without him, if all I had was prayer, I'd be dead. So I guess I'm in a strange mood tonight. Lots of questions. Doesn't feel like a good place."

I paused. "And I wasn't sure I wanted to say all this, but we are committed to walking together from wherever we are. So that's 'where I are.'"

I paused again. "I guess where I really am is a little afraid you'll all get sick of my mood swings and tell me to take medication just to make me easier to live with."

The mood turned instantly thoughtful. I was relieved. Had someone tried to "help" me with assurance of his or her patience or with empathic support or advice to get more balance in my life or to see another doctor for my headaches, I would have internally bolted from the room.

Bill looked concerned. Lisa was pondering. I could feel Rachael's tenderness. Scott put his face in his hands and thought. Margaret sipped her coffee. Jane said nothing. Richard spoke.

"That same fear sometimes keeps me from talking in this group. You all have been so supportive as we've struggled with our son. I could talk about more hard stuff with him every time we get together. Part of me doesn't want to, because I already feel your support, and I don't know what good more talking about it would do. But part of me does want to say more, and even to explore what's going on in me and Margaret as we try to parent this kid and keep our sanity; but I'm afraid, just like you, Larry, that you all will get tired of hearing about it again."

After a moment, Margaret said, "I wonder what it would mean to be a really safe group."

For the next thirty minutes, we thought together about whom we had felt safe with in our lives, and why. It was good conversation, an appetizer of SoulTalk before the main course.

We had been together an hour. Jane still had said nothing. Then, almost in passing, she offered, "You guys know what a struggle it's been for me to lose weight. And you've been so excited for me when I lost thirty pounds over the last six months. I really thank you for that. Some people get jealous. But the last month, I've been eating handfuls of M&Ms. I feel really angry, and I've put on a few pounds. I'm really discouraged. I guess I'm a little afraid, too, to bring that up."

Each of us heard Jane. The same mood of genuine care that I had earlier felt was now extended to her. The rhythm of the group flowed toward Jane.

"I didn't know you weren't losing weight anymore."

"I'm glad you feel safe enough to share that."

"That's got to be frustrating."

All good words, but none that entered Jane's battle. The group moved on to other things. We weren't sure where to go.

When Jane spoke, something had registered in me. I found myself thinking about her as the conversation turned in other directions. I couldn't get her off my mind.

To myself, I was asking, *What is the real battle here? What would make a real difference on her journey? Does all this Old Way versus New Way stuff fit here? Maybe she needs a good dose of accountability. Or are there deep wounds that need healing?*

I found myself wondering if an awakened desire for God had any relevance to where Jane was struggling. A few minutes later, with a mix of curiosity and confusion, I said, "Jane, can I ask you a question? I can't get what you said off my mind. I'm not sure if you want to say more about your frustration with weight, but if you do, I'd love to hear. My guess is we all would."

Transcendent curiosity that emerges from *thinking beneath* is open-ended. You just want to hear more. No hypotheses, no explanations, no effort to figure anything out, no point to make or help to give—just a desire to hear more.

Jane paused, smiled a bit nervously, then simply said, "Yes, I really would like to talk more. I'm scared, but I want to."

Silence. Warm, inviting silence, for about twenty seconds.

"Scott knows how frustrated I've been. He's been wonderful. Just this morning, he said something that really made me think. He said that maybe I was really furious that this whole thing is such a struggle. That really registered. I wanted to go on a diet, reach my goal, keep on with a whole new way of eating and exercising, and move on to other things. It hasn't worked that way."

Put yourself in the room. Can you hear yourself *thinking empathy, solutions,* or *help?*

- "Jane's really discouraged. I'd like to just hug her."
- "She's pretty unrealistic if she thinks problems go away. She might need a good dose of reality and learn to accept it."

- " 'Be not weary in well-doing' comes to mind."
- "This must be so hard for her. I wonder if she really hates herself from some of the wounds I know she felt from her parents. I'd like her to face those and maybe receive some healing prayer."

We didn't say any of those things. Because Margaret was *thinking beneath,* she said, "Something's going on in Jane that's going on in all of us. I wonder what her real battle is."

Scott, Jane's husband, looked up. He, too, was *thinking beneath.* "I want to read something from *The Message* in Romans 8. I read it just this morning and it really struck me that Jane and I both fight the battle Paul talks about here."

We all listened while Scott read. None of us said so, but we sensed the Spirit was beginning to move in our midst. We felt expectant as we heard Scott read: "The law always ended up being used as a Band-Aid on sin instead of a deep healing of it. And now what the law code asked for but we couldn't deliver is accomplished as we, instead of redoubling our own efforts, simply embrace what the Spirit is doing in us."

Scott paused, feeling some emotion. Then he continued. "Those who think they can do it on their own end up obsessed with measuring their own moral muscle but never get around to exercising it in real life. Those who trust God's action in them find that God's Spirit is in them—living and breathing God!"

Jane was staring at her husband as he read. At this point, she quietly said, "Wow!" Scott continued. "Obsession with self in these matters is a dead end; attention to God leads us out into the open, into a spacious, free life. Focusing on the self is the opposite of focusing on God. Anyone completely absorbed in self ignores God, ends up thinking more about self than God. That person ignores who God is and what he is doing."

The room was quiet. We had just led with our ears to hear from God. It was better than *lectio*. We were silenced.

Then Jane spoke. "That describes me. My diet began going bad the day after Marcy scheduled her wedding. All I could think about was how I'd look as the mother of the bride coming down the aisle. They're going to get married in three months, and my mind was totally focused on how badly I wanted to wear a size 8 dress. That's when I felt the pressure. I've been so absorbed with me that I haven't even thought about our daughter, let alone God. I wanted so badly to look pretty."

The group was fully engaged. We were ready for SoulTalk. We wanted to arouse Jane's desire for God.

Before I report what happened next, reflect on what's happened to this point.

As several of us shared our struggles and fears, Jane felt safe enough to mention a "journeying reality" in her life, both her recent weight gain and her discouragement. I earlier had let the group see some ugliness and insecurity in me. Richard revealed similar struggles. And none of us felt judged. Vulnerability in one creates a safe environment for another to be vulnerable.

I felt prompted to enter Jane's battle. Neither Richard nor I demanded that the rhythm of the group move toward us. We really didn't want that to happen. When Jane shared, we felt invited. We sensed an opportunity for SoulTalk was presenting itself. By *thinking beneath*, we tuned in to whatever was happening beneath her journeying reality. I happened to be the one who opened the door to let all of us see the battle.

The group pondered what the battle might be, with no mood of judgment toward Jane. The battle was in all of us. We were simply curious, transcendently curious, about how the battle had taken shape in Jane and how we could put words to it.

Scott felt prompted to read from Romans 8. God's Spirit had prepared him for this evening by directing Scott to that passage earlier in the day.

Jane meaningfully recognized the contours of the central battle raging within her as God spoke to her mind through Scott's reading of the Word. She could see her real problem was not a psychological wound that needed healing or an irresponsible laziness that deserved rebuke. The battle was being fought between the Old Way and the New Way—between her flesh, with support from the world and the devil, and her regenerate spirit, energized by God's Spirit. A second thing (looking pretty at her daughter's wedding) had become a first thing. She was valuing a legitimate good as though it were the greatest good.

The story of her soul was beginning to come into focus. She was committing spiritual adultery, becoming intimate with her desire for self and betraying her desire for God. Because she is saved, her "new nature," her appetite for God, was present and able to be awakened. The joys of brokenness were stirring in her soul.

What happened next was an epiphany—defined by my *World Book Dictionary* as "an appearance or manifestation, especially of deity; a sudden revelation or perception; an insight into the essence of a thing."

For the next hour, we spoke SoulTalk with Jane. We entered her particular story with transcendent curiosity. And the Spirit moved through our words to stimulate Jane to love and good deeds (see Hebrews 10:24). Second things that had become first in her affections were put in their place. She left that evening with a stronger appetite for God, still a struggling pilgrim on a long journey, but a pilgrim who had encountered God and wanted him more than ever.

I'll tell you how it happened in chapter 14. But first, I want to develop the idea that how we tell our stories can block the Spirit's work and get in the way of epiphanies. Like Jane's.

13

LISTEN TO HOW A STORY IS TOLD

Tuning In to the Energy behind the Story

STORYTELLING MATTERS. A close friend wept as he told me how ashamed he was to make known to me a specific failure in his life. "This is so hard. I can't believe how I've let my sin isolate me from everyone. I just couldn't bring myself to tell you what I've been hiding so long. And I wouldn't be telling you now except that I've finally had to admit I have no power to stop doing what I've wanted so badly to believe I could stop any time."

My friend is a highly skilled professional who for years has challenged my emphasis on the importance of telling your story to at least one person. More than once I've heard him say, "I just don't see the value in getting specific about what's happened in the past or what's happening inside now. I've certainly shared with you when I've felt discouraged; we all need encouragement from time to time. But what's the point of dredging up all this junk? I agree with Paul—forget what's behind and move forward. If we just walk in the Spirit, we won't need to worry about all those deep hurts and problems."

Denying your emotional past gets in the way of developing present intimacy.

He's thinking differently now. He realizes that when you cut yourself off from your story, when you make a point of not paying attention to the present effect of past events, you open your heart to profound self-deception. You risk deepening both your blindness to how you impact others and your resistance to understanding your own weakness and dependency.

Denying your emotional past gets in the way of developing present intimacy. And it blocks the flow of God's power in your life. Pretending that the past is over and done with, that its effects do not linger, preserves the illusion of independence. "I'm not hurting. I'm doing fine. I can just trust God and keep moving ahead."

THE FIRST MAN WHO CRIED "I"

Perhaps no single book has more powerfully communicated the importance of looking deep into your own soul and revealing what you find to others than Augustine's *Confessions*. Before A.D. 401, the year Augustine published his memoirs, no one other than biblical writers had so honestly told his or her story. One historian claims that Augustine's *Confessions* "are the first genuine autobiography in human history."[1] It reads like a narrative of pain. For example, he said, "I carried inside me a cut and bleeding soul, and how to get rid of it I just didn't know. I sought every pleasure—the countryside, sports, fooling around, the peace of a garden, friends and good company, sex, reading." What a description of second-thing living.

Augustine continued, "My soul floundered in the void and came back upon me. For where could my heart flee from my heart? Where could I escape from myself?"[2]

No one except biblical writers like David and Paul had ever written like that before. And no one had ever told the story of his or her soul in such shame-filled detail. Appreciatively, author Thomas Cahill dubbed Augustine as "the first man who cried 'I.'"[3]

Since then, of course, since Freud and the advent of the therapeutic culture, everyone cries "I." It's now the expected thing to do.

But with this difference: Augustine told his "I" story as a narrative of failure and pain within a larger narrative of grace. And that kept him from the modern habit of presenting oneself as a victim to be pitied. He viewed the story of his soul with transcendent curiosity. Like Jane as she told her story to our group, Augustine saw his life as a transcendent drama, a battle to the death between the forces of evil and the powers of good. We're more likely to see ours merely as a battle to feel better.

When Augustine described his sexual addiction, he did so

without whining or blame shifting, with no sense of noble struggle that merits applause or cynical resignation that calls for pity, and certainly with no lighthearted trivializing. No book more effectively teaches how best to tell the story of one's soul.

I hear him saying (and I paraphrase), "My most searing pain comes from my sin. I will not hide the ugly truth from myself or anyone. I will not cover my shame behind my position of prestige, my intellectual talent, or my considerable influence. I am what I am, an abject, perverted, helpless moral failure."

But the narrative of dark honesty is told as a prelude to the story of bright grace. How like the apostle Paul. Again, I paraphrase what I hear Augustine saying: "One day I awoke to the sounds of heavenly music, and I was filled with the joy I had looked for in every place but God. And it was this sovereign joy that lifted me out of the world of pain and into the universe of grace. Before I was moving in step with the relentless noise of hell. Now I found myself dancing in rhythm with the Trinity."

TELLING OUR STORY

We must tell our story. SoulTalk will come to an abrupt halt if we tell only the *facts about our life*. We must learn to tell the *story of our soul*, and we must listen as others tell theirs.

It takes some practice. One pastor of small groups arranged for a group of close friends to experiment with storytelling. He had caught the vision of forming groups dedicated to intentional spiritual formation and believed that knowing each other through storytelling was essential to the process.

After a six-month trial, he wrote me a letter:

Dear Larry,

Now what? We've all told our stories. We've made known what's happening in our lives and we've shared some secrets, some pretty awful ones, from our past. And people listened well. We didn't hand out quick advice, we didn't avoid hearing bad things by offering to pray, and, except for a few occasions, there wasn't much syrupy empathy. None of that "Oh I bet that's hard" stuff.

We asked questions. We reflected on what we heard each other say, and we even tried to listen to the Spirit to see if we could hear what he might be saying.

It went nowhere. We sort of enjoyed the process, but now we're frustrated. We don't see that it did any good and we don't know what to do now. Should we go back for another round of getting even more gut-level candid? To be honest, no one has the energy for that. I think we're missing something. I'm not sure if we're getting this "transcendent curiosity" thing. Is there some different way to tell our stories that we don't know? Any suggestions?

Well, I do have a few. And they've been stirred by Augustine. Before Augustine, no one in classical times told his or her story quite like he did. And when storytelling became popular in modern times, people didn't follow his example.

Since 1895, the official starting point of the therapeutic culture when Freud published *Studies in Hysteria*, people have told their stories as narratives of pain more than failure, and they have been looking for recovery, not redemption.

Now, with the rise of the postmodern (and to me, welcome) emphasis on authenticity, community, and discovery of identity in the stories we share, we tell our stories (and this I don't welcome so eagerly) as narratives of seeking, questioning, doubting, and deconstructing, in order to come together to experience the presence of others alive with iconoclastic hope.

If the core weakness of the therapeutic culture's way of telling stories is its blatant and shamelessly prized narcissism, the core weakness of postmodern storytelling in the secular world is the absence of the larger story of grace, of rebellion against divine order and redemption at divine cost.

Listen to the way most of us tell our stories today. We tell them as a narrative of tragedy, romance, irony, or comedy, none of which is a transcendent drama. And none of which invites the listener to listen with transcendent curiosity. Consider the various ways Jane could have told her story.

TRAGEDY

Jane could have told her story as a tragedy: "This weight thing is just awful. My mother was overweight. The odds are stacked against me. It's probably a genetic thing. I just don't see where prayer or the Spirit's power fits in at all. It's just going to be a lifetime struggle, I guess."

Think back to Tim Burke. He could easily have told his story as a tragedy: "Man, I don't get it. I gave up millions of dollars in income as a pro athlete to adopt five kids. And look what happened. I'm trying to stay faithful, but it's hard."

A woman leaving my weekend conference on SoulCare stopped long enough to tell me her story. It was told as a tragedy. "I'd love to have someone I could talk with in the way you describe. But it's about impossible to get into a group that's willing to do it like that when you're a divorcée. And I don't want to get with a bunch of other divorcées and just gripe. I'm really leaving your conference feeling pretty low."

Tragedies are the tales of people who identify themselves as victims.

Tragedies are the tales of people who identify themselves as victims. "Life has been unkind to me. I'm struggling to keep on moving, but it's tough. I can see nothing beyond my pain and the unfair-

ness of my world. I deserve your support. More than that, I demand it. But a lot of good that does. I think you should empathize with my struggle and be there for me and do whatever you can. Oh, I know that's selfish of me. It'll never happen anyway. So I'll just do my best. I'll keep trusting God and try to be nice to people. *I am a victim.* There is no greater truth than that. My life is hard, and it will stay hard. Don't be curious. Feel sorry for me and help."

ROMANCE

Some people have gotten the idea that they are the stars in a romantic story, heroes that merit recognition and deserve notice.

Jane could have told her story like this: "With all the odds that were stacked against me, it's a wonder I don't weigh four hundred pounds. I think the secret is to stop thinking so much about yourself, to stop feeling sorry for yourself and get busy. I've gotten involved in volunteer work at nursing homes, and boy, does that make you grateful for what you have. This current new struggle with weight is probably just a blip on the screen. I'll just stay busy. I'm actually visiting an old lady who's dying. I'll be going over to sit with her from midnight till six. She never sleeps well, and it means the world to her when I'm there. I'll be OK. I imagine I'll be losing weight again soon."

Tim's story lent itself to a romantic rendering. "Institutionalizing four of our five kids has taken a pretty big hit on our finances. We had a lot of money, but we're not rich anymore. Well, it's worth it. If we can just help one of these kids, I'd be glad to go broke."

Heroes enjoy pointing to their noble achievements. "See what I've done. I've earned the right to be heard. Because of my perseverance and determination, I've made it in the face of tremendous adversity. I should be on the lecture circuit.

Applaud me. Gather round to hear what I have to say. I've made it. *I'm a hero.* There is no greater truth than that. It's been hard, but look what I've managed to do. Don't be curious. Be impressed with me, and say so."

IRONY

This style of storytelling is becoming more popular in our postmodern culture. Remember the married couple sitting in my living room when the husband confessed to adultery?

Listen to how the wife might have told her story, tinged with tragedy and romance but focused on irony. "I can't believe what he's done to me. I'm sure I've failed too. I'm not the easiest person to live with. But I've done nothing to deserve this. And even if he stops his sexual fooling around, I'm still not sure I want him back. I really don't like him. He can be such a slob. I never feel like he's even thinking about me. So maybe we'll just live together. I guess it could be worse. You know, I don't know if anything really works. I get so sick of all those people who pretend everything's fine. At least I've got a couple of girl-friends who are honest enough to admit their marriage is a disappointment too."

People who tell their story as irony see themselves not as surviving victims or noble heroes, but as sneering cynics. Ordinary people fall for all that religious hoopla and noise. They think the latest method of counseling or healing prayer or the new conference led by Christianity's freshest star will do the job. "If you realize that nothing works the way it's supposed to, meet me for coffee. Let's speak honestly from our intellectually superior perspective so we can enjoy 'inner ring' fellowship. I am one who sees. *Realism has made me a cynic.* There is no greater truth than my realization that nothing in this life works well. There is no peace. Everything is meaningless. If you agree, let's talk. Don't be curious. Join me in my cynicism."

COMEDY

By far the most common way we tell our stories is as comedy. Just get on with it. Pull yourself up by your bootstraps. Don't dwell on your troubles. See the glass as half-full. There's always something to enjoy. Life may not be a bowl of cherries, but there's always a tree with a few ripe ones to pick.

Successful people specialize in this form of storytelling. For years, my friend who finally confessed his failure to me, the one I mentioned at the beginning of this chapter, saw his life as a religious comedy. He didn't view everything as funny—his life had its share of hardships—but he used Christianity to stay positive.

"Sure, things have been hard. I've got a couple of really hard things going on right now. But God is with me. The future is bright, if not tomorrow, then heaven for certain. I spend a lot of time in the Word. I'm in Ephesians now. I'd love to share with you what I'm seeing. It's unbelievable. Oh, by the way, did I see you driving a new car? That's great. Do you like it?"

Comedy tellers stay busy, distracted by religion and activities and responsibilities from reflecting on their lives for more than a few minutes. "Life is too short. Why waste time moaning and grumping? C'mon, God loves you. What more can you want? *I am a clown,* one who smiles his way through life. There is no greater truth than our opportunity to trust God and keep smiling. Let's get together for a good time. I love to laugh. Don't be curious. Let's just enjoy life together."

LISTEN WITH TRANSCENDENT CURIOSITY

It's difficult, but you can listen with transcendent curiosity to someone telling his or her story as a tragedy (I'm a victim; support me), a romance (I'm a hero; applaud me), an irony (I'm a cynic; sneer with me), or a comedy (I'm a clown; laugh with me). SoulTalk looks intently for evidence of the real battle and puts it into words.

"Tim, I would guess that the way life has turned out creates a lot of tension in you. You thought God would bless you for giving up your baseball career to adopt five needy kids. Now that life has fallen apart, you want to quit. Is there anything else you want than for your life to get back together?"

Every person's life is a transcendent drama, whether he or she sees it that way or not. There is a battle going on beneath the surface of every story. And there are two simple keys to recognizing and entering that battle. First, realize there is always a *hidden story* beneath every shared story. Second, the hidden story always includes *shaping events* that taught the person wrong definitions of life and gave shape to how he lives his life.

A few comments on each and we'll be ready to resume the story of Jane's epiphany.

First, the hidden story. No one tells all. To keep our life intact in our own strength, we must deny our deepest longings and our deepest guilt. When we own up to what we most want, we are brought into painful contact with emptiness and disappointment. We do not have what we were created to enjoy. We were made to experience perfect communion with God and profound intimacy with people in a thoroughly pleasant world.

Our communion with God will remain imperfect till heaven. Our intimacy with people, even in our best relationships, is flawed. And our world is filled with an uneven mixture of pleasant things and unpleasant, even horrible, things. Therefore, to be honest is to groan, to feel empty, to become deeply unsettled.

Facing up to our deepest guilt is even more disturbing. The unfaithful husband felt instant relief when he came clean about his sexual failure. In his mind, the next steps were obvious. He would never sin again like that, his wife would forgive him, and he'd return home as the loving and respected head of his house.

When I suggested his greater guilt had nothing to do with immorality, he felt uncomfortable. The realization that we've never truly loved another, even a spouse to whom we've remained faithful, puts us in touch with our terror of rejection. When I face my core sin, that I am more concerned with my immediate sense of well-being than with glorifying God by loving others, I feel desperately hopeless.

So we don't allow ourselves to become silent enough to experience how profoundly disappointed we are with life in this world and how far short we fall of what we know we are called to be and to do.

It requires the Holy Spirit working through a safe person, one who has already faced up to his own disappointment and failure, for others to share the hidden story of their unsatisfied desires and wretched guilt. But it is only then that they can tell their story as a transcendent drama. It is only then they can begin to see the battle between trying to make life work and drawing close to God.

Looking for the hidden story, the denial of desire and guilt—that's the first key in entering your friend's transcendent drama, no matter how she tells her story. The second key is to identify *shaping events.* As we'll see when I tell the rest of Jane's story, it can be a powerful experience to see how painful events have shaped our under-standing of death and how pleasurable events have shaped our understanding of life. When we're *thinking story,* SoulTalk will express transcendent curiosity about earlier experiences that were so painful we resolved never to feel that level of pain again.

> **Looking for the hidden story, the denial of desire and guilt—that's the first key in entering your friend's transcendent drama.**

SoulTalkers will be curious to know what experiences felt so wonderful that, for a moment, one's soul felt completely satis-fied, and a purpose for life—to feel that way again—was birthed.

In a SoulTalk conversation, I asked a friend to tell me when he felt most alive. He smiled and said, "When I brought my nine-day-old adopted daughter home from the hospital." He has been living ever since to recover the delight of that day. The girl is now sixteen. She feels smothered by her dad's constant attention. He is losing the battle. He is an Old Way parent and believes he is loving his daughter well. He is not.

As we've traced together the shaping events of his life, going back into his childhood where his deepest joy was caring for his younger sister in a single-parent home with an alcoholic mother, he has begun to see that what he calls "loving his daughter" is in reality his attempt to fill his own soul. He is making the shift from the religious Old Way journey to the spiritual New Way journey. The first step is spending less time with his daughter and developing other interests.

There is nothing more harmful to the soul on its journey to God than living an unobserved life. Learning to listen with transcendent curiosity as someone tells his or her story is important. It matters. It can move someone into the presence of God. It can create the opportunity for an epiphany.

It did for Jane.

14

MOVE TO THE CENTER OF THE STORY

Following the Spirit into Action

I LIVE FIFTEEN MINUTES FROM COLUMBINE HIGH SCHOOL, where two teenage boys opened fire on their classmates. Two days after the killings, I was standing in front of a television camera for a Christian network, invited by the producer to offer my commentary.

"What would make these young men do something so terrible? What does this say to us about the nature of evil and what we can do about it?" The news anchor was genuinely troubled.

I replied, "We'll not get far in understanding what went wrong with those young men until we recognize the same seed of evil in ourselves. As long as we sit back in horror and try to figure out their problem and what we can do about it without first recognizing the same fundamental flaw in ourselves, our theories about evil will remain comfortably shallow. We'll speak of poor socialization, peer pressure, uninvolved parenting, genetic defect, or the influence of media, music, and movies—anything but the radical self-centeredness that, except for Jesus, would keep all of us out of heaven."

"Cut!" At first I thought I was going on too long. I quickly learned that wasn't the concern.

The anchorwoman was indignant. Her eyes were flashing. "I would never do what those boys did. I'm incapable of killing another human being. I would hope you are too. How dare you suggest otherwise! Those two young men were evil in a way I'm not. Thank you for your time."

With that, the crew packed up and left.

As I mumbled an awkward good-bye, I thought about how Jesus shook up the religious audience of his day. Listen to what he said, and picture him repeating it on camera two days after Columbine: "You're familiar with the command to the ancients, 'Do not murder.' I'm telling you that anyone who is so much as angry with a brother or sister is guilty of murder. Carelessly call a brother 'idiot!' and you just might find yourself hauled into court. Thoughtlessly yell 'stupid!' at a sister and you are on the brink of hellfire. The simple moral fact is that words kill" (Matthew 5:21–22).

Earlier, Jesus had told the same audience what condition of soul was necessary if they wanted to experience peace, if they wanted good passions to be aroused in them that would keep bad passions—like killing people with words or bullets—in check. Here's some of what he said:

> You're blessed when you're at the end of your rope. With less of you there is more of God and his rule.

You're blessed when you feel you've lost what is most dear to you [second things]. Only then can you be embraced by the One most dear to you [first thing].

You're blessed when you're content with just who you are— no more, no less. That's the moment you find yourselves proud owners of everything that can't be bought [the pleasure of dancing with the Trinity].

You're blessed when you've worked up a good appetite for God [the purpose of SoulTalk]. He's food and drink in the best meal you'll ever eat. . . .

You're blessed when you get your inside world—your mind and heart—put right. Then you can see God in the outside world.

You're blessed when you can show people how to cooperate instead of compete or fight. That's when you discover who you really are, and your place in God's family. (Matthew 5:3–6, 8–9)

How could Jesus make himself clearer? He looks at tired, worn-out people who in their desperation and rage feel justified in doing whatever relieves their pain and tells them, in dramatic language, what must happen for them to become whole. He makes plain what must happen in our interior world if we are to restore broken relationships and experience emotional healing.

But we don't believe him. Let's ask ourselves:

• Do we want to get to the end of our rope? Wouldn't we rather have backup resources we can draw from—a sense of humor, self-confidence, good friends—when life gets rough?

- Do we really want to lose everything we hold dear? As one woman said to me after a class I taught on first and second things, "I've got about fifty things I'm clinging to. I'm willing to let go of several, but all of them? That's hard."

- Are we content with who we are, with the shape of our nose and the extra folds on our neck? Do we really think our joy does *not* depend on how we look at our daughter's wedding or how extravagant a reception we can afford?

- Do we actually want God more than anything else? Do we honestly believe we'd know real joy if we had him and nothing else?

- Are we so convinced that aligning our beliefs and desires with God's value system is so important that we devote priority energy to making it happen, even if it requires fasting, seasons of solitude, and denying ourselves the pleasures we can afford?

- Do we value cooperation to the extent that we neither compete nor fight—even when someone threatens our well-being?

We could say yes to all those questions, *if we were in a community where SoulTalk was the spoken language.* But it will not be spoken until we're broken. Until we realize that what was needed for the Columbine shooters, Eric Harris and Dylan Klebold, to become truly good people is exactly what is needed in our lives. Our passion for God must be awakened till it becomes the controlling center of our life. It never happened for Harris and Klebold. And it won't happen for us without SoulTalk.

IGNITING GOD'S POWER
THROUGH SOULTALK

Imagine how things could have been different if a classmate of the Columbine shooters had been *thinking beneath* and had seen the real battle raging in those two image-bearing but Old Way–controlled souls. Suppose a committed young man had *thought vision* and had written each of the two boys a letter describing the qualities he saw in them and how those qualities could develop. What would have happened if this school chum had been aware of how turned off he was by Harris and Klebold's punk attitudes and fascination with dark culture but had yearned to move toward them with the energy of Christ?

Perhaps a conversation would have occurred in which the angry young men might have made known to this friend how enraged and alone they felt. Perhaps their SoulTalking friend would have responded with transcendent curiosity rather than rebuke or retreat. Perhaps the Spirit would have opened Harris and Klebold's eyes to realize that the enemy of their souls was getting the upper hand.

Our passion for God must be awakened till it becomes the controlling center of our life.

Things might have been different. Or they might not have been. SoulTalk is not a magic formula for changing lives. But it does provide opportunity for the Spirit to move deeply into hearts where the devil is winning.

I don't naively believe that if someone had just been nice to those two boys, if someone had simply understood their pain, that some mythical goodness in them would never have been corrupted. That's nonsense.

But I do believe in the power of the gospel. When Paul declares the gospel to be the power of God (see Romans 1:16), he is not referring to explosive power, like dynamite. The Greeks knew nothing about gunpowder. Paul realized the good news of God was itself a divine energy, poured into human hearts through Christ-resembling relationships, in which the truth of God was taught and the life of God was lived. And that's SoulTalk.

I also believe that the mysterious and sovereignly miraculous power of God's Spirit could have introduced those boys to a New Way to live that would, had they embraced it, have led them in an entirely different direction.

And I believe that same power is required for me to walk in the New Way. Because I am a follower of Jesus, that power is in me. But it can best be ignited through SoulTalk.

Is the gospel powerful enough to have transformed Saddam Hussein? Had the divine energy of Christ reached into Osama bin Laden's soul on September 10, 2001, is it possible that the events of September 11 would never have happened? Is there any other power that could have changed his insanely wicked heart?

Why am I not cruel in the way Saddam was? Why would I never fly planes into the Twin Towers? Why is it unthinkable for me to imagine myself opening fire on a seminar audience I am addressing? Is it because I am a naturally better person? Or is it because the divine power of God entered my soul? I am what I am only because of the gospel. There is no room for pride or self-congratulation. The cliché is true: I must look at Saddam Hussein and other truly evil people and admit, There but for the grace of God go I.

JANE'S STORY CONTINUES

Jane is no Saddam Hussein. By the power of divine energy, she is a lovely woman. Her heart belongs to God, not fully, but meaningfully. She's still an internal mess, like Billy Graham and your pastor and you and me, but she is a devoted and good mother, a loving and faithful wife, and a caring and wise friend.

And yet she remains capable of killing her daughter's soul by worrying more about fitting into a size 8 dress than being there for her daughter on her wedding day. What's wrong with her? The same thing that's wrong with Saddam Hussein, Osama bin Laden, and the Columbine shooters.

"Where do you think all these appalling wars and quarrels come from?" James asks (James 4:1). Why did Saddam kill to maintain power? Why did I feel so mad at the guy in my Bible class who for several weeks in a row challenged my teaching with what felt to me like a smug attitude? Why did Jane think more about wearing a certain size dress than about her daughter's joy?

James answers, all these evil thoughts and actions "come about because you want your own way" (v. 1). This inspired writer was of the opinion that our problems arise from our commitment to Old Way living—decide what you think you need and go after it. You "fight for it deep inside yourselves," in a place that can only be accessed when you tell your story and reflect on what's happening with the help of someone who speaks SoulTalk, someone who is transcendently curious when you make yourself known.

James continues, "You lust for what you don't have and are willing to kill to get it" (v. 1). Thomas Aquinas once remarked that only two courses of action are open to us: Either we live to get a good we think we need, or we live to enjoy a good we've already been given.

When Scott read to our small group from Romans that "obsession with self . . . is a dead end," Jane realized that she was living to get a good she didn't have. That's when she quietly said, "Wow!" That was the beginning of brokenness, the same brokenness that could have transformed the Columbine killers into model citizens—had someone spoken SoulTalk.

Let me tell you what happened next in Jane. I wish it had happened in Klebold and Harris. She had just caught a glimpse of the real battle she was fighting. It wasn't with weight; it was with the Old Way. "This whole darn weight thing went bad when I started thinking about how desperately I wanted to look good at my daughter's wedding. The image of myself as a pretty woman represented life for me. I have no idea why—I think it goes deeper than seeing models on the cover of fashion magazines—but I became obsessed with it. I don't think God is anywhere near first place in the middle of all this. That's awful!"

When we see a friend experiencing brokenness, it's easy to see nothing but self-hatred and low self-esteem, and to want to affirm, "Jane, you are already pretty. We love you just as you are. And so does God. Right now he is singing over you with delight. He sees you as beautiful, and so do I."

Lisa meant well by speaking those words, but she was trying to help, to fix Jane. She was not dancing to the Spirit's rhythm. Brokenness needs to be entered so that the flow toward repentance follows. Instead, Lisa tried to make a point that she wanted Jane to hear, a point she hoped would help Jane by affirming her.

Jane was unmoved. "I know that's right. And I appreciate your saying it. But—and I wish it were different—I just don't feel the impact of what you say."

To her great credit, Lisa responded, "I think I spoke too soon. I just so badly wanted you to be free from this need to be slender."

There is a huge difference between *thinking vision* and requiring solutions. The first looks ahead to what will be but isn't now. The second insists that what could be happens now.

I followed up on Lisa's good comment by suggesting, "Let's picture ourselves at the wedding. Jane has just taken the usher's arm and is starting her walk down the aisle. What do we most want to see happen?"

"Well, it sure has nothing to do with what size dress she's wearing." We all laughed at Bill's remark. Jane laughed too.

Margaret offered, "I'd love to know she was so caught up in God's love and her daughter's joy that she'd feel at peace with who she was."

Rachael added, "There's something about being in control that robs lots of women of real rest. I'd want to see Jane taking no responsibility for anything except enjoying the moment."

We sat quietly for a moment. Then Jane spoke. "I can feel a shift in me." Pause. "I can actually picture myself walking slowly down that aisle just so grateful that I know God. And looking into each of your eyes and feeling his love." Jane began to softly cry.

At that moment, I could feel something happening in me I didn't like. I was *thinking passion.* That's what follows *thinking vision.* When you realize what you want to see happen in another, you begin to see what is happening in you that could block the flow of Christ's life out of your soul and into the other person.

I was aware that the evening was going well, and I felt proud of my contribution. My spirit sagged. "Oh, Lord, I can't do anything well without feeling proud. If I keep talking with this going on inside me, I won't dance. I'll step on Jane's feet. My impact will not be good, no matter how clever my words might be."

Out loud I said, "What are each of you feeling right now? I'm aware that this conversation is going really well, and I'm a little proud of my part."

Scott replied, "I was just thinking that my wife might be easier to live with."

Richard said, "I couldn't think of anything to say. I guess I was feeling inadequate. I'm not sure if I know how to join the conversation."

Jane smiled. "It's so good to know you're all as big a mess as I am."

We all relaxed.

Bill looked thoughtful, then said, "I felt like hugging Jane or all of us gathering around her to pray. But that feels premature. I think there's more to her story than we've heard."

Notice the flow. It's not a formula, but it is a spiritual rhythm that releases the language of the Spirit: from *thinking beneath* ("Is that the battle?"), to *thinking vision* ("What could the Spirit do?"), to *thinking passion* ("How am I getting in the way?") to *thinking story*. The cycle repeats itself, perhaps many times, until the desire to *think more story* moves someone toward reflecting on her hidden story and the shaping events it includes.

Jane was quiet. I asked, "What memories do you have where, maybe with a boyfriend or your parents, you felt bad about your weight?"

She thought for a moment, and then a light went on. She cleared her throat and said, "When I was eighteen and getting ready to go away to college, I realized I had put on some weight. The clothes I was packing were a little tight. It really freaked me out. I had always been thin and here I was, about to enter a whole new world, and I was getting heavy.

"I remember bursting into tears. It must have been pretty loud, because Mother and Dad came racing into my room to see what was wrong. I ran to Daddy and said—and I remember my words—'Daddy, I'm putting on weight and I hate it.'

"And I *clearly* remember what he said. 'Look, if you want to lose weight, eat less. What's the big deal? Do you think you need a psychiatrist or something?' Mother said nothing. They both just left.

"I was devastated. He wasn't allowing me to struggle. I felt so invalidated. And I remember making a decision. I would handle whatever came up in my life by myself. Because if others saw my struggles, they might respond like Daddy. And that would really hurt.

"I guess I defined life as being able to handle everything, to be in control. This is strange, but I really feel good talking about this. My soul feels lighter. It really does. That shift I mentioned earlier seems more real now. I can feel how much I want to just enjoy my daughter and help make her day really special. I still hope I lose weight, but that seems more like a second thing now. I feel less pressure and more freedom to lose weight.

"I really do feel released. Released to think about God more than about me. And to be who I really am. To be me. What God says, and what you guys have been saying, seems more powerful than what Daddy said."

That, friends, is an epiphany.

THE RHYTHM OF SOULTALK

I began that evening with a headache. I ended it with joy. We had just seen the power of SoulTalk. I want you to see it, too, to experience it more and more as you talk with people you love. It will require that you dance. I don't want you to miss the supernatural rhythm, the four dance steps that gently directed the flow of our conversation.

First, Jane shared a journeying reality. "I'm putting on weight."

Then, the group began to *think beneath.* We thought about the real battle going on beneath the weight concern.

As Jane's battle between the Old Way and the New Way came into view, we felt more dependence on God's Spirit to do anything about it. With dependence came confidence. We could *think vision:* What did the Spirit want to do in Jane?

That led us to *think passion:* What energy within us was competitive with the divine energy of the gospel?

Brokenness over our internal passions and hope for the vision that was emerging freed us, not to think solutions, but to *think story.* With transcendent curiosity we heard that Jane's recent weight problem came back when her daughter's wedding was scheduled.

That led to going through the cycle again: What's the battle? What's God's vision? What in us is getting in the way? Then we could *think story* more deeply. Then Jane remembered the incident with her father when she was eighteen.

As Jane owned her sin of determining to stay in control and to never again experience what she was wrongly defining as death, she felt released. That's how it happens. Looking bad in the presence of love releases our true self. And our interior world shifts to resemble the interior world of Jesus a little more. God reveals his grace through a SoulTalking community. Perhaps in an epiphany. And we move toward the vision of spiritual formation.

And that brings us to the fifth and final dance lesson: *think movement.* How does the Spirit move us from where we are to more closely resembling Jesus? That's our next topic.

15

LEAD OTHERS TO A NEW LIFE IN A NEW LAND

Embracing What the Spirit Is Already Doing

Can broken relationships really be restored? Will deep wounds from your childhood ever be healed? Does anyone ever come to the point where he or she actually feels more excitement about God than about having close friends or seeing his or her kids do well? Do you know anyone who truly experiences joy when life is turning south?

Remember Heather? She tried to teach me how to dance. She promised more than she could deliver.

So does religion. You've heard the siren's call:

- "Here's the right way to raise your kids!"
- "Is your marriage tense? Follow these six proven keys to intimate communication. You can have a great marriage."
- "Has your level of self-contempt reached the boiling point? God can put things back in order. Let me show you how."

The religious way feeds on self-obsession. The goal is always the same: *You can have the life you want!* Nothing matters more. Blessings that make us feel good are the point. Communion with God, experiencing him in a way that lets us share in the joy he feels, is sweet talk. But that's all it is; just talk. The real world is all about *me*.

C. S. Lewis put his finger on the problem with religion when he said, "Put first things first and we get second things thrown in; put second things first and we lose both first and second things." Religion makes a nasty habit of putting second things first.

LIVING IN THE NEW WAY

But there is another way to live, a New Way. And people all around the world are finding it. Not many, but a few in every continent, a few in every country, a few in every church. But it takes just a few to touch the many, to get a revolution in relationships under way, to open the door to a radical shift in culture.

We *can* leave behind the religious journey. We *can* repent of our penchant for obeying God to coax him into making our lives better. We *can* set out on the spiritual journey.

Of course you want your daughter to remain a virgin till she marries. But don't shower her with wholesome hugs and affirming comments in order to keep her chaste. That's putting second things first. That's religious parenting. That's the Old Way. That's falling short of treasuring God above all else.

Do all the same things, but do them for a different reason.

Hug your daughter to reveal God to her, not to keep her out of bed with her boyfriend. That's your prayer, but it's not your responsibility. You can't control her choices.

There is all the difference in the world between parenting your children in a certain way because you are obsessed with God, because you long to reveal the source of your deepest joy to them, versus parenting them according to a plan that is designed to mature them into delightful young people. The second way, the Old Way of the written code, puts pressure on both you and your kids—on you to get it right, and on them to meet your expectations.

You're working hard, and they better shape up: That's the formula for rebellion or compliance, for your kids experiencing a false but exhilarating sense of personal freedom through rebellion or deadening their souls to please you.

The New Way honors your children's dignity, it takes their sin into full account by recognizing the law isn't the cure, and it invites them through God-revealing firmness and grace to feast on the food they long to enjoy but don't know where to find. Parenting on the spiritual journey disciplines without getting caught up in power struggles, it teaches with respect for freedom of choice, and it loves without requiring your kids to fill your emptiness. It relieves them of the need to be your god.

A NEW JOURNEY TO KNOW GOD

Since my battle with cancer, I have been on a new journey to know God. The epiphany that the Spirit gave me in that hospital room (described in the introduction to this book) has become my Damascus Road experience. It was not my conversion—I converted to Christ a half-century ago.

But it was my awakening. Suddenly I felt joy. Curing my cancer instantly became a second thing. The Spirit picked me up and placed me on the spiritual journey. I still wanted the surgery to be successful, but that hope faded into second-thing importance compared to the prospect of running freely about in heavenly places, breathing celestial air, and dancing. Oh, what a dance! Moving in rhythm with the Spirit, leaping in the redemptive power of the Son that never fails, and falling into the welcoming arms of my grinning—yes, *grinning*—heavenly Father.

I am now persuaded that either we shift to the spiritual journey, or we will continue in the mists of self-deception.

Never before had I known so personally what it meant to join the eternal party. And the vision came in a hospital room, when I was facing the very real prospect of losing everything but God!

Since then, it's made sense to me to value every second thing I desire as a second thing, to literally want all the good things of life less than I want God. I understand and resonate when I hear an observer of modern civilization remark that the twenty-first century will be spiritual or it will not be.[1]

From the depths of my being, I am now persuaded that either we shift to the spiritual journey, desiring God more than the good life, or we will continue in the mists of self-deception, walking a way that seems right; and we'll end up losing both the experience of God in this life and, inevitably, the good life we worshiped.

My biggest mistake as a parent was to love our two sons too much. When each was born, I immediately added him to my list of first things. I didn't see it; the mists of self-deception formed a thick dark cloud in front of my eyes, and what I thought was godly love for them was really narcissistic love for me. I was caved in on myself as I went to their ball games, coached them in tennis, disciplined them firmly, and taught them the Scriptures.

Seeing them turn out well—a legitimate second-thing desire—became a key piece of the good life I was convinced I needed in order to know joy. My religious journey as a parent was an exercise in self-worship dressed up to look like godly fathering. I was a fool.

Now I am a zealot for SoulTalk. Here's why: *I am convinced that the language God longs for us to speak is the most powerful tool we have to follow the Spirit's movement in the human soul.*

He is moving in each of us to lift us off the religious path and onto the spiritual path, to shift us from Old Way living to the New Way to live. And he's moving in us because he loves us. He is obsessed with Christ because he knows Christ is life, the source of everything good. He wants to release his power through us to lead others to a new life in a new land.

When we're living that new life, the Spirit takes great delight in restoring relationships, healing wounds, deepening passion for Christ, and giving joy that nothing can take away. These blessings are all second things, but things the Spirit longs to provide, *after* our appetite for Christ becomes consuming.

Heather didn't teach me to dance very well. My wife's toes are safer now, but no one turns to watch. No one taps me on the shoulder and says, "Will you teach me to dance the way you dance?"

It wasn't Heather's fault. She was a good teacher. The problem is in me. I simply lack the kind of rhythm that releases my arms and legs and shoulders and head to move in sync to good music.

Heather was a good teacher. Just like God's law. His Ten Commandments teach me how to live. As a follower of Jesus, when I hear his instructions, I *want* to obey. I really do. Just like I wanted to dance well.

But there's something wrong. I seem to more easily move in step with the devil's noise.

- When I feel criticized, I get defensive.
- Where expectations exist, I feel pressure.
- When I think someone doesn't like me, I sulk. Following the devil's lead, I imagine getting even, and I feel hellishly alive with vengeance.
- When I hear about a party I wasn't asked to attend, I want to throw a party of my own and not invite the host who snubbed me.
- When I feel hurt or neglected or disappointed, I can think of no greater injustice than what I'm suffering. So I

fight for justice, for my cause. And I wonder why you don't join my battle to recover my sense of being and value and worth. Well, of course you don't. You really don't care. Nobody does.

And then I tell my story, first to myself then to anyone who will listen, a therapist if necessary. I tell it as a tragedy: "Look what I have to endure."

Or, if I feel feistier, I tell it as a romance: "I'm emerging out of the rubble life dumped on me, and I'm doing it with heroic strength. Applaud!"

Sometimes the joys of smugness and superiority are the best ones available. So I gather a few disillusioned friends and we enjoy great fellowship in darkness. We sneer at life together. My story becomes an irony.

I might, however, get so sick of feeling bad that I vow to feel better. So I quit pouting. I play golf or go shopping or volunteer to teach fourth-grade Sunday school or give myself to work or buy a new car or join the country club or throw another party or go to the church that makes me feel best. Any distraction I can find. And my life becomes a comedy, with me starring as a clown who paints on the smile and lives happily on the surface of life, as far above the pain and emptiness in my soul as I can get. Oh, I share my struggles—for five or ten minutes. Then I suggest we run out for dinner and a movie.

That's how I naturally live, in one of those four ways. You do too. So the question becomes, How do we move from whatever form of self-obsession we're living to the God-obsession of the New Way? How do we want to dance with the Trinity more than wanting them to straighten out our life?

LIVING UNDER THE OLD WAY

Under the Old Way, we won't be able to dance with the Trinity. On the religious journey, our teacher is the law—watered down, so we have hope of keeping it. But we still can hear its demands, and somewhere deep inside we're convicted. We know we aren't measuring up to God's standards. From the top of Mount Sinai, we hear music with a rhythm we can't follow.

So we give up, we deny our guilt, and we do our best. We live our life in the energy that we naturally feel, not realizing that our natural energy aims toward second things. It values health and friends and money and family and satisfaction and joy and adventure and romance and meaning—more than it values God.

Borrowing some lines from Paul in Romans 1 and 2, I can describe my natural energy as a passion that leads me to treat God shabbily, to refuse to worship him, to trade in his glory, the One who holds the whole world in his hands, for "cheap figurines you can buy at any roadside stand" (Romans 1:23).

No wonder I have trouble dancing in rhythm to heaven's music. My natural energy leads me to think there's a better way to live than knowing God, and it blinds me to the consequences of such a foolish and evil idea. Chasing after some pleasure other than God makes me forget how to be human. Corruption sets in. The image of God remains part of me, but it's spoiled. Perverted passions flare up. I become addicted to whatever pleasure I can reliably control, which sets me to running in circles after my own tail, never realizing how silly I look.

While all this is happening in me, I somehow manage to put on a good face. I become a "good-enough" Christian. I sign off on an orthodox statement of doctrine. I pride myself on not sinking into certain forms of visible sin, like you-know-who. And I keep up with church attendance. I might even tithe and volunteer for the evangelism committee.

Without recognizing it, somewhere deep inside my soul, where no one can see, all hell breaks loose. I grab and I grasp. I viciously backstab, but I do it in a way my friends enjoy. "We need to pray for her. Did you hear what she's doing?" I bicker. I cheat. I kill with words. I resent authority when it interferes with my freedom, just like a three-year-old who yells, "I hate you, Mommy!" when it's time for bed.

Something even deeper inside than this dance of hell tells me I'm heading in a wrong direction. But I can't stop. And for a while, I really don't care. I'm on a dark spiral downward, and I really think you should understand and reach out to me, not to rebuke me, but to support me, cheer me up, to walk with me, and help me feel better without telling me to change course.

That is the dance of hell. Millions of Jesus followers are dancing it. And our program-rich, success-driven, excitement-addicted church culture doesn't see it for what it is. It slaps a Band-Aid on surface wounds and ignores the deadly cancer that's spreading.

- Have devotions!
- Get involved in a small group!
- Tithe!
- Join the choir!
- Read the latest Christian bestseller!
- Sign up for that conference!
- Pray more!
- Pray this prayer, not that one!
- Be Reformed, not Armenian!
- Follow Wesley, not Calvin!
- Raise your kids according to the Bible!
- Take your teenager on a dad-and-daughter date!
- Talk to your budding adolescent son about sex and drugs!
- Get counseling to heal your wounds, to recover your damaged self!
- Speak your wife's language of love!
- Stop holding a grudge against your husband!
- Stop being so negative!

And the real battle in the human soul is never entered. No one speaks SoulTalk. The battle between the Old Way and the New Way is not even recognized. No vision for what the Spirit longs to do in our interior world ever becomes clear. No one sees the self-obsession that is polluting our internal well, that keeps living water from pouring out of our soul into the thirsty souls of others.

We never listen to another's story. And we never tell ours as a transcendent drama to a soul friend, to someone who leads with transcendent curiosity. Our hidden story of shame remains untold. Embarrassing secrets are never shared. Real struggles, our real failures, are never seen. We mingle with Jesus followers every day and continue to live the very real tragedy of an unobserved life.

THE DELIGHT OF A SOUL FRIEND

Now, turn around. See the sunlight. Imagine a friend walking toward you while you're still in the darkness, still dancing to hell's music.

Imagine a soul friend, what the medieval Irish called an *anmchara*, a person you could trust for a lifetime. They had a saying: "Anyone without an anmchara is like a body without a head."

Stretch your imagination. Let this person who enters the devil's dance hall be fluent in SoulTalk, someone who:

- *thinks beneath*, who sees your real battle between the Old Way and the New Way, who knows the difference between the false gospel of religion and the true gospel of Christianity;
- *thinks vision*, who looks at you with eyes brimming with hope, eyes that see your uniqueness and believes in who you could become;
- *thinks passion*, who is self-aware and therefore humble, who is so broken that he is confident in the Spirit, and when you're with him, you catch a whiff of Jesus, and the fragrance is sweet;

- *thinks story,* who patiently endures as you tell your story—as a tragedy, romance, irony, or comedy; someone who listens with transcendent curiosity and therefore can see a soul looking for God in all the wrong places, a friend whose eyes glisten with love as he rebukes and confronts and exposes, whose voice drips with grace as he directs and invites, whose words carry unshakable hope as he explores the story of your soul.

Now imagine *yourself* as that friend, entering the battle for the soul of someone you love, speaking the language God longs for you to speak.

In your relationship with the person you love, the teacher is no longer the law. You are no longer Moses' representative issuing commands. Principles to follow are no longer the theme of your conversation. The Holy Spirit in you both is now the teacher.

The law, of course, remains. It will forever. But not now as a written code chiseled in stone and held over our heads by a stern lawgiver. No longer do you want your friend to tremble before Mount Sinai. Now you're approaching Mount Zion, the city of God, together. The law is in you both, written on your new hearts. What used to be a holy obligation is now a holy desire. Now you want to do what you ought to do, and you long for your friend to enter that freedom. It's his to enjoy.

Now you want to love God by obeying him. You want to love your spouse by giving up pornography and grudge holding. You want to parent your kids in order to reveal God to them. You want to serve your friends and be a good citizen and build your community, because you want God's will to be done on earth as it is in heaven. And you know your friend wants it too. These desires may be buried in your friend's soul, but they're there.

You no longer come across as a self-righteous crusader against abortion and strip clubs and gambling and child abuse and prostitution. You no longer command fellow Christians to join you in moral battles and to go to church and to support their pastor and to love their families. And yet you're more meaningfully and more firmly than ever against the bad and for the good.

But now you spread the aroma of Christ, inviting people to a better way by speaking SoulTalk. Now you hear the music of heaven and you realize that the Spirit's rhythm is in you. It's really there. And now, when you hear the music, you start dancing. You can dance the dance of heaven, the same dance the Trinity has been dancing for a million years, and then some. It's the dance that will go on for eternity with no one ever dropping out in weariness. It's the dance that you and I and the people we love can dance now!

OUR CONTINUED STRUGGLE

We'll never dance like pros till we get home. We'll still miss the rhythm and step on a few toes. There's still something in us that likes to move to hell's noise.

Like Paul, we must honestly admit, "I'm full of myself—

after all, I've spent a long time in sin's prison" (Romans 7:14). Apparently, Paul had a story to tell too. And like us, it included both a *hidden story* of shame and *shaping events* that caused him to misdefine life and death till he met Jesus, and beyond.

Paul B.C. (Before Christ) was a master of religion. He followed more than six hundred religious principles scrupulously and felt quite proud of himself. Paul A.D. (After Damascus) was on a spiritual journey. But like each of ours, his journey didn't always go well. And in Romans he invites us to listen to a snippet of his story with transcendent curiosity. "What I don't understand about myself is that I decide one way, but then I act another, doing things I absolutely despise" (7:15).

Paul! You too? That comforts me. Paul, you didn't give up hope, even when you failed. And you persevered through seasons of incredible loss. You lived your whole life after Damascus expecting to dance perfectly one day and dancing pretty well during your life on earth. How did you manage to do that?

"I need something more! . . . I realize I don't have what it takes. . . . Something has gone wrong deep within me and gets the better of me every time" (vv. 17, 18, 20).

You really do struggle, don't you, Paul? What's the solution?

"I've tried everything and nothing helps. I'm at the end of my rope" (v. 24).

Paul, didn't the Master tell us that we're to consider ourselves blessed when we get to the end of our rope?

Of course. When I'm at the end of my rope, I finally ask the right question, which is this: "Is there anyone who can do anything for me?" Isn't that the real question?

So you're saying we can never live the New Way that you mentioned in Romans 7:6 as long as we're self-obsessed. When we get to the end of our rope, we realize our self-obsession offers no hope, and we're open to becoming obsessed with God. Is that what you're saying? Is that the answer?

"The answer, thank God, is that Jesus Christ can and does" lead us into the freedom of God-obsession. "With the arrival of Jesus, the Messiah, that fateful dilemma"—living the Old Way while desiring to live the New Way—"is resolved." Now we can *simply embrace what the Spirit is doing within us*" (Romans 7:25; 8:1, 4; emphasis added).

And we can do it best together, in communities of folks who speak Soul-Talk. We can lead each other into a *new life in a new land.* And we can do it by embracing what the Spirit is already doing in us.

That's the fifth and final lesson in SoulTalk: *think movement.* The Spirit is already moving into our battle, toward a vision of what we could become. He is moving through broken brothers and sisters into our soul, when stories are told to transcendently curious ears.

And when we discern the Spirit's movement, we can follow

> **When we get to the end of our rope, we realize our self-obsession offers no hope, and we're open to becoming obsessed with God.**

along. We can speak words that highlight and energize and release his movement.

Let's think about that. Let's *think movement.*

16

Don't Jitterbug to Beethoven

Speaking in Rhythm with the Spirit's Movement

When you dance with the spirit, he takes the lead. Always. The moment you move more quickly or in a different direction, you're dancing with yourself. And you're speaking SelfTalk.

It happens all the time—from pulpits, in counseling sessions, through books, at seminars and conferences, over coffee with friends, in small groups. SelfTalk is an epidemic, more common than AIDS and just as deadly. Here's how it happens.

A problem comes under discussion. Perhaps it's divorce or depression or discouragement. Something isn't going as we wish it would. We hurt. We're upset. We're unhappy.

The focus immediately becomes *solution:* What can we do about this? What strategy can we implement to get us back on top, to feel about our life the way we would like to feel? How do we resolve all this suffering and see blessings restored? What is

God's plan for making things better? And we ask all these questions claiming that we have God's glory in mind, not realizing that we are reducing his glory to his provisions, not his person.

That's the thinking behind too many sermons. That's the direction we too often follow in conversations with troubled friends.

We are a blessing-obsessed culture. We live for blessings, and we disguise our self-obsession and its underlying spirit of entitlement with God-talk. God wants us happy. God hates divorce. God loves to bless. An appreciation for his kindness subtly shifts into self-entitlement. If God didn't withhold his only Son, can we imagine he would withhold any good thing?

Then we define "good things" as whatever second things we want the most and trust God to provide them now or at least soon, certainly in this life. Blessing-obsession. Self-obsession. Second thing—obsession. It's all the same. And it blinds us to what God-obsession really is and what it would look like in our lives.

PUTTING SECOND THINGS FIRST

The weakness of modern Christianity, with its shallow worship and rootless excitement and crowd-friendly relevance, can be traced to one assumption: *We think God's Spirit was sent to earth to give us the happiness that blessings bring.* The suffering Lamb has done his work. Now the mighty Spirit has taken over. And his job is to build on the finished suffering of the Cross by overcoming our problems, healing our wounds, setting things right, and replacing suffering with adventure, meaning, and romance.

Now we're in competition with every other religion and self-help movement and political ideology to produce the good life. It's a competition we cannot win, because Christ never promised us the blessings of heaven till we get there.

As a Christian culture, we have put second things first. We are in immediate danger of losing an authentic experience of God and in eventual danger, because of our self-obsessed spirit of entitlement, of losing the legitimate second things God wants to give us, things such as a spouse who loves us and kids who live responsibly and friends who relieve our loneliness. God may or may not give us these good blessings, but if we put first things first, we will come to know him. That is the first thing. And one obstacle to his granting second things will be removed.

God may or may not give us these good blessings, but if we put first things first, we will come to know him.

We rightly believe the Spirit is moving. He is. All the time. In everyone we speak with, and in us. But we assume he's moving on a timetable we set (weekend conferences that promise emotional healing by Saturday night) and in a direction we choose ("This weekend you will feel his touch, and it will restore your soul. It will fill you with joy." Could the Spirit instead be promoting an experience of emptiness *now* to create space, which he will later fill?).

The danger of SelfTalk disguised as SoulTalk is never greater than when we *think movement.* Modern Christianity has dramatically reversed its ancient form by assuming that the Spirit is moving toward giving us a good life (as we define it) more than growing Christ in us. We therefore devote our primary energy to helping ourselves and others live happily and well, and we do it in the name of Christianity. As a result, we speak religious SelfTalk. It happens in most churches in the Western world every Sunday. SelfTalk abounds.

But if we think biblically about where and how the Spirit is moving, opportunities for true SoulTalk much more abound.

You'll soon be chatting with someone you love. You're preparing to teach Sunday school or lead your small group or preach a sermon or meet someone for coffee. You've led with your ears as people have shared their stories. Perhaps you know a little of their hidden story and a few particularly powerful shaping events.

And you've been *thinking beneath* the stories you've heard. You understand the battle between the Old Way and the New Way, and you recognize it in yourself and others. In dependence on the Spirit, you've *thought vision.* Your heart is stirred by what could happen in this person's life. And you continue to monitor your internal motives to check whether you want to feel important or whether you're afraid that you're not important. Either way, you're humbled and repentant. You long for the Spirit's energy to control and empower your words. You've *thought beneath,* you've *thought vision,* you've *thought passion,* and you've *thought story.* There's more thinking to do in each, but you're ready for the next lesson.

You want to make a difference. You want to see people move

toward the Spirit's vision for them. You're not demanding it. To do so would elevate "making a difference" to first-thing status. Your only first thing is to enjoy God and reveal him to someone else, to discern then follow where the Spirit is heading. But you want to know what you can do to partner with the Spirit in promoting change. You're ready to *think movement*.

You know you have something to say if you speak SoulTalk. You know you might be used of God to deeply impact the life of a family member or friend if you speak the language God longs for you to speak. God could use you to restore a marriage. Or he might not. Either way, your life will make Jesus Christ more attractive to all with eyes to see, and God's joy will deepen. But you still long to see movement in the person you love. It's a second thing, but the desire for it is legitimately strong.

Nothing is quite as thrilling as actually watching the Spirit move in front of your eyes. And nothing is quite as satisfying as knowing that the words you speak are catching the wave and rolling with the Spirit to shore.

THINK MOVEMENT

Let me introduce our fifth dance lesson—*think movement*—by telling a story. It's a true story, one that begins in years of sadness and pain and moves into a new life in a new land.

Marlene's husband left her four years ago. He was marrying another woman in a month. Marlene told her story to a group of us who had gathered for a week to move together into each other's life in rhythm with the Spirit.

"There's a family occasion coming up next weekend where my ex and I will be together. I don't know if I want to ignore him, tell him off, or just be coldly courteous. I know all that's wrong, but I really don't know what I'm supposed to do."

Whenever you hear the word *supposed*, notice it. The word has no rhythm, only obligation. It's an Old Way word. Marlene continued.

"If I'm to flow with the Spirit's movement when I see him next weekend, I'll need a lot of prayer. Right now I'm just scared. And angry. And pretty hurt." She wanted to move from the Old Way to the New, but she knew that would take a miracle.

Our group had spoken that week about the real battle going on in all of our souls, of wanting our lives to work well and wanting to feel good about ourselves, and desiring those legitimate blessings so badly that they'd become first things in our affections. We confessed that as long as second things were first, we would come undone if they were not granted. We'd fall into bitterness, revenge, and self-protection.

We talked about spiritual formation, how the Spirit detaches us from dependence on blessings by letting us feel the pain of losing them and having to face how strong our spirit of entitlement is. Then the Spirit helps us discover the deep empty space in our soul that no second thing could ever fill. Only God.

We had spent time looking into our souls to discover the deep yearning that no restored marriage or any other blessing could satisfy, and we reflected on what it meant to actually experience God as our satisfaction, even without the blessings he could provide.

Fourth-century theologians painted a picture of God that they hoped would give people a vision of what it would mean to fellowship with God, to enjoy the experience of communion with him. They came up with the word *perichoresis*, which literally means to dance around—*peri* means around, as in perimeter, and *choresis* is from the same root as choreography. The Trinity, they suggested, could be properly envisioned as dancing together in the perfect rhythm of love at a wildly exuberant party.

As a group, we imagined the Father pouring into the Son, delighting in Jesus with absolute freedom knowing there was nothing in the Son that would ever displease him. We pictured the Son yielding himself with carefree abandonment to the Father, filled with sheer devotion to the Father's beauty. And we envisioned the Spirit forever exploding out of the profound intimacy between Father and Son as the eternal Third Person in the sacred dance.

Saturday morning, our next-to-last morning together, we worshiped as one of our members danced before us, inviting us by the beauty and charm of her movements to join the Trinity in their dance. Then a gifted pianist, another of our group, let her fingers fly over the keys of a grand piano, and we all left our chairs. For perhaps fifteen minutes, we danced together, in rhythm with the beautiful music that filled the room.

No one swayed. We *danced!* And our dancing followed the majestically wild and reverently free music. It was a sight to see. Older folks, younger folks, outgoing folks, reserved folks, slender folks, chubby folks, tall folks, short folks—we all danced, *together.* Unique but united. Joined in celebration.

Caught up with rhythm from without that resonated with rhythm from within.

Twenty-four hours later, during our final morning together, we prayed for Marlene. After our week together, we could sense the direction the Spirit was taking her. We knew he is so obsessed with the Son, whose deepest joy is to reveal the Father, that he wanted Marlene to count it a happy privilege to reveal Christ's character to her ex, to dance before Jim in the rhythm of divine passion.

Two weeks later, our group received this letter. I quote it only in part, with a few of my editorial comments in italics and with a few changes in identifying details.

Dear Precious Friends,

I have so much to tell . . . thank you so much for the prayers that you were sending to the throne. When I was in church last Sunday, I realized I needed to see my ex's mother. So I called her after church and she said to come on over. We had a great talk . . . she said several times that the divorce was her son's fault.

Without the Spirit's nudging toward God-obsession, how easy it would have been for Marlene to eagerly agree and to let that comment stoke the fires of bitterness.

By Monday morning, the comment she made about the divorce being Jim's fault was bouncing around in my head and screaming for notice.

Was the SoulTalk of the earlier week bearing fruit? Was God answering prayer?

All the time, maybe all the past week or more, I had been praying not my agenda, but your agenda, God. As I walked the dog, I remembered an incident that happened in the first year of our marriage.

The Spirit brings to mind whatever hidden stories or shaping events we need to remember to clearly see what passion is ruling in us today. In her letter, Marlene describes an event where her husband persuaded her to join him in the kind of place that should not exist. At the time, neither Marlene nor Jim were Christians. But Marlene didn't want to go, hated it, and was mocked for her reaction.

As I went to that memory, I realized that he had a choice— reject me and my reactions or deal with it and acknowledge there was something wrong with him . . . guess which he chose. But the biggest thing is that I chose sin too.

When memory recall is directed by the Spirit, there is a compelling awareness of where the Spirit is taking someone, and there is an awareness of sin that is stronger than an awareness of pain. The effect is brokenness. The result is the release of spiritual energy that restores the soul. That's healing. That's what happened in Marlene.

I chose to respond with anger and rejection [back then]. But this day I was filled with the compassion of Jesus for this man . . . I was flooded with such mercy and grace toward him. And I spent some time crying and mourning the choices we both made to protect ourselves. Then the Lord showed me the depths of my sin.

The Spirit's movement is always toward the vision of our interior world resembling the interior world of Jesus. Nothing interests the Spirit more, not our blessings, not our comfort, not even our happiness. And the process always begins with brokenness over the realization of how unlike the Lord we are. When we see our sin, we are broken. And living water flows through the cracks.

It was fathomless! I was completely undone by the ways I had not loved Jim, not supported him in his career, acted as though I didn't care about him in countless little ways, even clung to my father instead of cleaving to my husband, all just to keep Jim and the pain at bay and make my life not hurt.

For years Marlene had valued feeling good over surrendering to God and so fell into the common sin of self-protection. But now she was convicted by the Spirit of living the Old Way, of treasuring the experience of less pain over closeness to God.

All morning I was overwhelmed with how much the Lord loves my ex and longs for him to dance with the Trinity. I realized what he is missing—what a PARTY he's missing! I went to the meeting [with Jim] with great expectancy and anticipation.

To restore her marriage? To use Marlene's stern love to convince him of his sin? Either of those outcomes would make for a good testimony in church. I can hear the applause had Marlene announced to the congregation that she and Jim were getting remarried. Religion would be celebrated: Get it right and God blesses.

But the Spirit was on the move toward what he values most, not a restored marriage or emotional healing but rather a disciple who counts it all joy to suffer for the sake of the gospel, a Jesus follower who begs God to bless her in a certain way but worships him when he doesn't.

When I got there, we ordered lunch. Then I started and asked him not to comment until I finished, because I wasn't sure if I could get through it otherwise.

Rhythmic dancing often starts with deliberate steps.

I related the memory in all its gory details. I told him all the ways I had chosen to respond to his rejection and all the ways I had sinned against him (that I could remember). I told him I forgave him for the choice he made and the many choices he had made during the twenty-six years of our marriage. I asked him to forgive me.

One who has been so badly and obviously sinned against can only ask for-giveness under the influence of God's Holy Spirit.

I told him that I wanted this to be a gift to him and his fiancée, that I had so much compassion for him and no hate or anger anymore.

Remarkable! Marlene slew the giant of pride within her and won the victory. There is no greater joy or greater privilege for the soul than to love Jesus as the first thing.

I think he was shocked. He said something about reconciliation, which made my heart move that direction. As he talked about his fiancée, though, I realized that it was not what I wanted or what the Lord wants for me.

I see no self-protective retreat here. I see only the miracle of a human will, previously self-obsessed, now falling in line with the divine will.

I told him I believed he is a good man and longs to be that. We laughed and shared some more things, and left together. He asked me if he could hug me, which I gladly accepted. It felt good for the first time in at least a decade to be hugged by this man.

One true measure of having first things in first place is the ability to enjoy whatever second things come our way, even when they fall far short of what we might have wanted. Every glimmer of beauty confirms that the rumor is true: There is a better world, and it's coming.

Then we said good-bye. Did God get the glory? I think so. I slept last night for the first time since coming home [from the week in the mountains with the dancing group] all the way through the night.

Another second thing, an especially welcome one, that came when she put first things first.

I'm rejoicing and dancing, interrupted by bouts of regret, repentance, and deep mourning.

Groaning and growth continue till heaven.

God is truly good . . . This morning as I was walking the dog, the Lord whispered in my ear, "I've set you free FOR something, not FROM something." I can't wait to see what he set me free for. I saw your prayers answered and even more than I could have desired or hoped.

Love,

Marlene

During our week together, our group spoke SoulTalk. We danced in rhythm with the Spirit's movement. It could have been different. We could have said, "Marlene, you've been hurt so much. Don't let him hurt you again. Treat yourself with respect. Establish boundaries to keep you safe. God doesn't want you to suffer anymore." Or, "Wouldn't it be something if you and Jim got back together? We have a big God. Let's trust him for big things. God wants to bring you out of the darkness of divorce and into the sunlight of a reconciled marriage. Let's pray to that end. Now, what could you do that would give reconciliation its best chance?"

There are countless ways to speak SelfTalk. And Christians speak them all, every day. But it's all self-obsession. We want what we think will bring us the greatest joy, and we want it now. So we jitterbug while the Spirit plays Beethoven. We frantically chase after what we think we need while the Spirit is softly and tenderly calling us home.

If we're going to *think movement*, we must be clear: The Spirit is obsessed with the Son. He wants nothing more than to see the Christ he knows and loves formed in Marlene's heart. Why? So she can join the dance! The Spirit knows there is no greater joy, for both the Father and his prodigal daughter.

And that's the first thing—to dance with the Trinity. That's what happened for Marlene. The group spoke SoulTalk, and the Spirit did the rest.

THE MYSTERY OF SOULTALK

Think movement! Fix it in your mind: The Spirit is moving in the moment as you speak with the person you love. Discern his direction, keep in step, and know what the journey in that direction will look like. Then you'll be speaking SoulTalk.

But be cautioned. There are some things we can understand, some truths we can know because God revealed them to us in the Bible. But what we can know will never serve as a manual for helping people change. Mystery will always exceed knowledge. There's no formula for SoulTalk, but if there were, it would be ten parts mystery to one part knowledge. Did we really think it would be different?

Can anyone explain what happened to Marlene? Can we reproduce it at will with someone else? We can, of course, talk about the process. I can come up with a verbal description of the soul's deepest battle and encourage you to look for it beneath people's problems. I can borrow from Paul and warn you that if you enter the battle in another's soul and develop a vision of what could happen, you will feel acute pain every bit as bad as childbirth.

I can urge you to pay attention to what's happening in you as you listen to another share his or her struggles, and I can tell you that until you see your sin as greater than any sin that has been committed against you, you will only speak SelfTalk. And I can discuss what it means to listen with transcendent curiosity, not only to what people say, but to how they say it, to how they tell their story.

But after I do my best, everything we learn together, everything we could ever learn together, adds up to one part knowledge. The rest is mystery. Nowhere is the "formula"—one part knowledge, ten parts mystery—more evident than when we *think movement.*

I invite you now, with terrifying and exhilarating dependence on God's Spirit, to enter the mystery of his movement. You'll find yourself in another world.

17

ENTER THE MYSTERY OF MOVEMENT

Finding the Courage to Cooperate with What We Cannot Control

I JUST NOW LISTENED to a voice message from Marlene. "Yes, you may use any part of the letter you want. It's amazing. Thirty years of anger toward this man—and now it's gone. I can't believe it."

When I heard her words, I felt relief, and surprised. *Wow!* I thought. *She really changed!* Oh me of little faith.

Another woman just called me. She, too, had received Marlene's letter. Listen to her reaction:

> When I read it, it really troubled me. I didn't know why, but something about what she said left me very uncomfortable. I couldn't stop thinking about it.
>
> And then it hit me. Marlene's ex had left her for another woman after years of rejection. When I read about that awful place he had taken her when they were first married, I was

furious. How could he do that to her—and then to ridicule her for not liking it. But as she remembered that terrible story and all the rejection she felt ever since, she saw *her* sin against *him* in the middle of all *his* sins against *her.*

Everything became clear. My husband sinned against me in the early years of our marriage. He rejected me when I was still trying to do everything I could to keep him loving me. For all the years since, it had never occurred to me until I read Marlene's letter that beneath everything I was determined to never be hurt like that again, and that my determination was wrong. It was just such a natural part of me, like breathing. If I gave it any thought at all, it felt justified. He was the sinner and I was the victim, and I was just trying to keep from feeling too awful.

After reading Marlene's letter and stewing over how bothered I was by something, I suddenly saw how badly I had wronged my husband. And I could see my fist shaking in God's face, asking him to help me not feel any more pain. I wasn't dancing with God. I was filing a complaint.

I've never been so happily broken. I felt eager to ask my husband's forgiveness, to tell him how wrong I was for not inviting him to the party, for thinking his sin was so much worse than mine. And when I did, he said, with a tenderness I loved, "I never thought I'd hear those words." Our relationship has taken a big step in a new direction.

As I listened to this woman's story, I felt humbled and ecstatic. With all my training and experience, I could never have moved this woman's soul to see her sin and to genuinely and joyfully ask forgiveness. But the Spirit could—and did. When we speak SoulTalk, we soon realize that without the Trinity, we can't do anything. And with them, we can only marvel at mystery and cooperate with a process we can never control.

Sure, I can articulate a few principles that emerge from Scripture and are borne out by the stories I hear. I can hold up a vision of what it would be like to join the Trinity in their wild dance. I can explain how a transcendent vision opens our eyes to see not only what is possible because of Jesus, but also what's getting in the way because of our flesh, to identify the buried sin that we thought was perfectly normal but is blocking movement toward the vision.

I can describe how true brokenness over personal sin is worlds different from agony over rejection, and how only the misery of brokenness, never the misery of rejection, frees us to seek God. In brokenness over sin, we seek God as our first thing, pleading for his mercy, not screaming for our rights (see Hosea 5:15; 7:13–14). And I can chart progress on the spiritual journey:

In brokenness over sin, we seek God as our first thing, pleading for his mercy, not screaming for our rights.

- from *brokenness*: "I've sinned against the one who sinned against me. My sin is as offensive to God as is his. And I've sinned against God by treating him like a second thing."

- through *repentance:* "I've been on the religious journey, trying to do what it takes to make my life work and to feel alive. I want to trade in all that self-obsession for God-obsession."

- into *abandonment:* "I'll follow the Spirit wherever he tells me to go because I am willing to risk trusting God, even when he does nothing visible to warrant my trust."

- toward *confidence:* "God's been dancing all along. And now I'm walking onto the dance floor. I can hear the music. Look! I'm actually dancing, and I feel alive. Communion with the Trinity is real and fills the center of my soul. This is life!"

- resulting in *release:* "Now I *want* to bless those who have hurt me. My pain isn't the point. Yes, I still hurt, but I'm becoming God-obsessed! I'm a little more like Jesus! And it's who I really am. I'm discovering my true self. This is joy!"[1]

And the release of who we really are as new creatures in Christ, as solid, alive, and joyful Spirit-led beings, often brings in its wake all manner of second things: restored relationships, whether with ex-husbands who marry someone else or with husbands who in new ways feel warmth from their wives; emotional healing from trauma that led us in wrong directions to find life; an aroused appetite for God that is felt even more deeply when dreams shatter; and a joy that no loss of second things can destroy.

I can write books and lead seminars and participate in small groups and chat with hurting friends in my living room, but when genuine spiritual movement occurs, when someone's interior world becomes more like the interior world of Jesus, all I can do is shake my head in wonder and worship, and say, "Oh, God! Look what you did. Thanks for letting me watch and play a part. Empower me to speak SoulTalk more often. I know it's the language of the Spirit, the language you long for me to speak."

SOUL TRANSFORMATION

Several times a year, New Way Ministries holds a one-week School of Spiritual Direction, a group of thirty people who gather for a week to walk together on the spiritual journey. Each school ends with a banquet in which participants share stories of the Spirit's movement. Tim Burke, my baseball-playing friend who adopted five special-needs children, attended one of these schools. He stood at the end of our closing banquet and, with tears, said, "I must say something. Can you stay for a few more minutes?"

Tim described the mystery of the Spirit's movement this way: "My pain over our family struggles has been so great, I've wanted to die. I've told God a thousand times I'd rather go back in time to when life was good. I knew I couldn't, so all I wanted was out. But now I see that all the agony I've experienced has opened the door to knowing God in a way I never have and never could have without the pain. I want to love my wife and my kids, and to serve God anyway I can. *I want to live!*"

Change that we understand is never miraculous. Change that we can reproduce at will is not supernatural. It may be good change, but it will not inspire worship. I swirl a capful of Scope in my mouth when I wake up, and my morning breath, which could kill a dragon, becomes fragrant. That's no miracle (though some mornings it comes close). A chemist could explain the transformation.

But soul transformation, from Old Way living to New Way living, from trotting along the religious journey to movement on the spiritual journey, is different. When God becomes real in our experience and first in our affections, you can be sure you've seen the hand of God.

When Marlene's anger of thirty years disappears, when a severely sinned-against woman reads Marlene's letter and is broken over her own sin, when a former baseball star who once had the world by the tail reports that very real despair has given way to hope, it's God. No one can explain it.

We can only look up and see the Trinity dancing. The Father is singing with delight. The Son stands by the Father's right hand, experiencing the joy that was set before him as he prepared to suffer. And the Spirit is whispering with quiet excitement, "Jesus gave you life. I'm stirring it up. Go! Enjoy the Father. Adore the Son. Dance with us! You'll have the time of your life."

As we look into the heavenlies and with the eyes of faith see the unseen world, we feel more certain than ever that SoulTalk is the language God longs for us to speak. Through SoulTalk, the Spirit moves people toward knowing God more intimately and relating to others more deeply. That's what life is all about—loving God and loving others, no longer with self-protective passion ruling in our soul, no longer self-obsessed and speaking SelfTalk.

I don't want to paint a too-rosy picture. Speaking into the mystery of movement requires courage. It can be confusing, especially when we deal with another's failure. Is now the time to promote brokenness by exposing sin? Have we thought vision enough so that we're not just scolding people for their selfishness? Are we dealing with someone else's sin in order to feel superior or perhaps as a concession to the legalism still in us? Or are we tingling with excitement as we anticipate the release and freedom that brokenness brings?

When God becomes real in our experience and first in our affections, you can be sure you've seen the hand of God.

While we're trying to figure out what it means to put God in first place, life continues on. A simple comment by our spouse enrages us; our son is caught with marijuana and we have to decide whether to sell his car or ground him or pray with him or explore his feelings. We don't know what to do. Plus we have bills to pay and laundry to wash and a lawn to mow and a job to handle.

The temptation to write off all talk of dancing with the Trinity as sweet thoughts that have no relevance to real life can become strong. But when we get serious about seeking God's presence over his blessings, two things happen. First, we begin to sense an inner strength, and perseverance becomes a possibility. Quitting doesn't feel necessary, no matter how empty and discouraged we feel. Second, wisdom sneaks into our soul. Here's how it happens.

When our appetite for God is the strongest desire in our soul, then certain courses of action we would have never before considered begin to seem right. The way that seems right to the God-obsessed person usually is right. If the way we *want* to handle a troubled marriage or a rebellious child falls within biblical parameters, then we can trust it, even when it flies in the face of culture. More than likely, it's the Spirit providing us with wisdom to navigate through life, not to make it better, but to reveal the character of God to all we meet. And some second things *do* get better.

THE JOURNEY OF MOVEMENT

I sat again last night with the couple I mentioned in chapter 7, the husband who confessed infidelity and the wife who was too numb to speak. It's been a month. We've met several times in-between, but this was a long conversation.

I did all I knew to do. I thought hard about the real battle they were each fighting. I put into words the wounds they each had suffered and their desperate determination to protect themselves from further pain. I painted a vision of what selfless, God-obsessed living would look like in the middle of their particular fights and tensions.

I kept close watch on my own internal world and could discern both an impatience that wanted to move things along faster and an Old Way energy that felt inclined to focus on practical tips to make things better between them. I listened to more of their stories. Both of them wept as they shared what was hard in their lives, and how disrespected and unnoticed they felt.

Think beneath, think vision, think passion, think story—that's what I can do. And when it comes time to *think movement,* I can do that too. I can think about brokenness with some wisdom and I can make observations that might promote it. I can think about repentance and abandonment and confidence and release, and I can exhort movement in the process. But actually *moving* someone into the New Way—well, that's another matter. It's out of my league.

In my mind, I can sketch this journey of movement—brokenness, repentance, abandonment, confidence, release—and I can sometimes discern where someone is in the cycle and what the next step would be, but I can never make it happen. I'm not in control of what matters most. I'm dependent on prayer, not cleverness.

Movement away from managing pain into the mystery of divine love is always a supernatural work. It's what the Spirit does.

My job is to follow the Spirit's movement, never to try to move people on my own. I am to desire the Spirit's goal for my troubled friends: not a better marriage, but an aroused appetite for God that could lead to a better marriage. I am to wait for the Spirit to move and then tag along, to walk through doors he opens into their souls, not to insist they see something now and change.

I am to prepare myself for the long journey ahead. The process of detachment from second things, things like protection against more pain and a demand that we feel our spouse's tenderness, is always rough. It always involves suffering. Ask Tim. Following the Spirit into the New Way in a new land takes us into a few dark nights. And when we're there, we wonder if we've taken a wrong turn.

I am to be there when the people I love begin to seriously ask if there's anything to this whole Christian thing. And I am to realize the questions become tougher the longer the journey continues. I am to know from experience that the path to joy moves first into the desert where nothing makes sense and then leads into the valley where the pain in our heart seems unbearable and unending.

I am to cooperate with this process I cannot control, knowing whatever my friend goes through is worth it, that no suffering is worthy to be compared with the joy of dancing with the Trinity.

If I join the Spirit's movement in someone's life, I will be given the joy of seeing another person join the dance. Like Marlene and Tim and Jane and so many others.

Thinking movement IS NOT A TECHNIQUE WE MASTER; rather, it's a relationship we offer, a relationship energized by the Spirit's passion and guided by his wisdom. Perhaps the best way to communicate what it looks like is to tell a story, a story just starting, where the outcome is entirely uncertain.

The Spirit is again inviting me to enter the mystery of his movement into another person's life and to draw from him the courage I will need to cooperate with a process I cannot control, a process that may or may not go well.

Let me share with you what goes on in my mind as I anticipate another opportunity for SoulTalk.

18

LEARN THE UNFORCED RHYTHMS OF GRACE

Waiting for God: A Final Story

FRIENDS CALLED about their sixteen-year-old daughter. She just admitted to an abortion that was performed a month ago. They had no idea she was sexually active.

"What should we do? Can you help? Would you speak with her, or with us if you think that would be better, or maybe with all three of us? Whatever you think would do the most good."

I wonder what they mean by "most good." Old Way thinking comes so naturally, especially in crisis. Nothing matters more than solving whatever problem has arisen. God's presence doesn't seem like the point, unless of course, he's willing to show up and use his power to straighten things out.

I felt instant pressure. How on earth did I get into this helping business? People seem to think I'm sitting by the phone waiting eagerly for the chance to take on one more set of troubles. I could feel myself getting irritated.

I tried to regroup. These are good friends. I do care about them. And I can't be too hard on them for wanting their daughter to return to a better path. If I were in their shoes, that's exactly what I'd want.

Do I really believe that's the Old Way? Do I really think the Old Way is bad? Of course they want their daughter to live well. Who wouldn't? Isn't that love?

Is it really possible to want something else more? All this talk about treasuring God above all else—what does that mean when your precious little girl is sleeping around? What does it mean when you visualize her sneaking off to an abortion clinic and letting a doctor kill her baby?

This is too much. I'm tired—tired of thinking, tired of talking. I'd rather pick up a novel and lose myself in an exciting story where bad people lose and good people win. I don't know what to do. Call someone who does. I'm taking a bath.

And I did, early that evening after I received the phone call. As I slid into the hot water, I could hear thoughts gently pressing for attention. I asked myself what it would mean for these conscientious parents to dance to heaven's music in the middle of their worries. What would it mean for me to keep first and second things in their proper order, right now, as I think about my reaction to my friends?

There is a time to not return phone calls, to not schedule a conversation with hurting friends. There is a time to waste a morning, productively, with a thrilling novel, or to play golf or to spend a quiet evening with your spouse or friends who are not in crisis. First-thing commitment to God does not mean that you never indulge second-thing desires. We are human. We do need a break.

As I soaked, I quieted my mind. I focused on the liberating truth that God is in charge, not me. I simply await orders from him. I discern his orders by sensing an internal rhythm that makes me want to move, not by doing what's expected, not by responding to what other people think I should do, not by determining where the most pressure is coming from and giving in.

Responsibilities matter, of course. I must pay my bills and file my taxes and keep my promises. I want to be responsible. There's rhythm in responsibility.

But it's frighteningly easy to think I'm being responsible when what I'm really doing is meeting other people's expectations and letting them pressure me into cooperating with their agendas. Then I'm taking my orders from them, not from God. I have several besetting sins. That's one.

As I lay in the tub, I could sense a genuine desire to engage with these distraught parents and their acting-out daughter. I may not have the time. My energy is limited. I get a lot of headaches. But I could feel an unforced rhythm carrying me into thinking more about them.

I *thought beneath*. Without knowing any details beyond what they had briefly shared, I knew the parents' biggest battle would be to live in the New Way of the Spirit and to regard their daughter's restoration as a second thing. That's hard. There is no more difficult battle. And it's a battle that can only be won by a supernatural power within us, fighting for us.

I knew the devil-inspired and world-encouraged flesh would rise up against the Spirit and rush these parents, with zeal that felt godly, into earnest prayer for their daughter, into endless talks that would soon disintegrate into blame games, into finding the right person to talk to who is trained and experienced in handling these sorts of problems.

Prayer is good, husband-wife dialogue is good, and talking to wise friends is good; but if all these good things are aimed at getting it right so life works better, it's the Old Way. It's the religious journey, energized by the flesh. And it will soon bear fruit that fits its source.

So the battle, the real one going on in each parent, would need to be entered.

I *thought vision.* I would love to see this mom and dad do what I didn't do, something I didn't even dream of doing when one of our teenage sons rebelled. For years, I had no higher priority than handling my son well and seeing him change. He felt the pressure and hated it. Anyone would.

I envisioned this couple doing better. I let my imagination loose as I tried to picture them more fully centered in Christ, more gracefully moving in rhythm with the Spirit, more God-obsessed with the Father's pleasure in view than self-obsessed with relief as their hope. Could they really enjoy what they already have in God so much that they would not desperately need what they badly wanted from their daughter?

I shook my head. The answer was no. Unless the Spirit moved and they followed. My vision was high enough to reduce me to dependence. I knew I was on the right track.

I *thought passion.* I could feel an angry pride surfacing into my awareness, tinged with a dash of self-pity. How nice if I could become the hero of the moment, like firefighters after 9-11. I could call these people back, offer to dive into the rubble of their lives, and pull them out before the debris smothered the life out of them. Then maybe I'd be properly appreciated.

It was a delicious thought. I might find an illustration for my next book or SoulCare conference, and under the guise of ministry, I could tell my story as a romance. I'd cast myself in the starring role, with appropriate caveats about giving God the glory, and I could present myself as a weary warrior who found the strength to win one more battle.

I indulged my fantasy for several seconds. Then I could feel the fear. What if I flubbed? What if they "tried me," then went to someone else with a different understanding of SoulCare who restored harmony to the family? I knew, I just knew, that God would not cooperate with my plans to be the hero!

Fear turned to resentment. God can be so maddening. These parents are weak. Their daughter is ignorant. And they're all stubborn.

Fifty years I've been following Jesus, and I still think like that. I shouldn't be surprised. The flesh will be with me till I die. And when I let it get the upper hand, it will bear its fruit—jealousy, pride, anger, and fear. *What a miracle,* I thought. *I can come like this to the Father, feeling dirty as a pig in mud, and he's always glad to see me.* That's the grace of reception, and it draws me to God.

And even this mess, all these self-obsessed thoughts and feelings that crawl like snakes through my interior world, can be put to good use. They're already forgiven. And facing them can lead to brokenness, which can then release the pure river that has been stopped from flowing through my soul toward others. *Everything leads me to Jesus.* I remembered those words from Jean-Pierre de Caussade, and I thought about the power of the blood. That's the grace of redemption, and it draws me to the Son.

There are better things in me than that. I really do love this family. I don't care if I'm the hero. Even if God uses me, he'll still be the hero. He always is. And that's really what I want. Yes, I'll get involved with this family. I feel led to do so, and it feels good. That's the grace of rhythm, and it draws me to the Spirit.

I climbed out of the tub, dressed, and sat by the fireplace to think some more. I felt peaceful and alive. I was dancing with the Trinity, enjoying the Father's grace of reception, the Son's grace of redemption, and the Spirit's grace of rhythm. My mind went to my friends with spiritual passion, no longer ruled by those awful passions of the flesh.

I *thought story.* What hidden story would I hear when we got together? There's always more than the journeying reality that is first presented. Much more.

Had the husband been unfaithful? Did he have a secret life of perverted sexual fantasy? Were his secrets filling him with shame that made him feel weak? Was he backing away from strong involvement with his daughter? Or perhaps he tended to be overly strict and even controlling to bolster his feelings of manhood.

What did his wife know about her husband and about herself? Was her tenderness locked in a vault so no one could betray it? Had she perhaps not been able to rest in her husband's strength and reacted by taking control of the household, including their daughter? Would I find the typical pattern of a managing wife and a disappearing husband?

And what about shaping events? If I led with my ears as a safe person, if I listened with transcendent curiosity, what would I hear? Did the husband feel believed in by his dad? What specific events had wounded him deeply, crushed his soul, and taught him the lie that death was failure and life was success? I know this man. He comes across as decisive, competent, eager to talk and share his opinions. Where did that style of relating come from? And what buttons does it push in his wife? And in his daughter?

Does his wife's background include abuse? When she told her husband about it (if she did), how did he respond? Did he pull the typical macho thing: "I'll kill that guy if I ever get my hands on him" (which, of course, makes the woman feel as unsafe with her husband as with her abuser)? Where did she feel deeply loved? Who is she pretending loved her more than they did? Her father? Her mother? Whose image is she protecting to keep from facing her loneliness and terror?

What's going on inside their daughter? How does she experience her parents? Exploring primary relationships is always more significant than exploring secondary relationships, and your relationship with your mom and dad is always primary, even when you're eighty. Parents are the first people every child turns to for what only God can provide. It's in that relationship that disappointment is deepest.

With these questions scurrying through my mind, I returned to *thinking vision*. The Spirit was not committed to giving these parents the magic insight that would change their daughter. He was committed to leading them into an experience of communion with God that would free them to move toward their daughter with a nonpossessive love, a love that was neither threatened nor controlling.

If the daughter felt that kind of love, the kind that keeps the Trinity dancing, she would be drawn. It's exactly what she wants. She might resist, but her parents would become a doorway into her soul through which the Spirit could enter.

I looked at my watch. It was late and I was tired, so I went to bed. I had done enough thinking about the battle beneath, about vision, about the ugly passions within me that reflected self-obsession and the divine passions within me that drew my soul more to God than to anything else, and about the hidden story I might discover and the shaping events that Satan used to persuade them that the life and death of their souls was not wrapped up in God.

I woke at five o'clock the next morning *thinking movement*. How did I expect the Spirit to move? He reliably surprises me, but I know where he's heading, and I understand a little of what is necessary to get there. Here's what I thought.

First, the parents must be still. Good dancing begins in quietness. Only when we're quiet can we hear heaven's music. No one ever leaves the Old Way and begins life in the New Way without first being stopped, as Paul was stopped by a blinding light on the Damascus Road.

SoulTalk would not give quick advice or provide empathy or call in experts. SoulTalk would say something like, "Before we talk about what you can do to help your daughter, tell me what all this trouble with her is stirring inside you." I would want them to reflect on the real battle being waged in the war zone of their souls before we concerned ourselves with the wise handling of their daughter.

Parents who are single-minded in their demand to "help" their children inevitably create power struggles. They might pray, read Scripture to their kids, take them away for a fun weekend together, send them to a counselor or to a rehab camp, dialogue empathically, and lay down clear boundaries with specific consequences. But as long as helping their children remains their first thing, it's all SelfTalk, no matter how much "Christian" wisdom it might reflect. They would be applying pressure and calling it love. They would be treating their children as God, depending on them for the experience of joy and mistaking it for Christian parenting. Internal forces would be stirred in the children that would arouse their flesh even more.

If their daughter were spunky, she might rebel, if only to prove that she is no appendage of her mom and dad. A more compliant type might yield to the pressure; she might change to please her parents and win their acceptance or to get them off her back. She might even rededicate her life to Christ and become a spiritual phony, a Pharisee with good behavior coming out of a bad heart. And her parents might thank God for answered prayer.

These parents will need to move to the spiritual journey, to live in the New Way of the Spirit. As they come to recognize the battle going on in their souls, SoulTalk might encourage them to kneel together and to surrender their daughter to God, to confess their idolatry of treating their daughter as if she were the first thing in their lives, if that in fact is what they're doing. I suspect it is. We all do it.

If I sensed the Spirit were leading, if the parents seemed to be flowing with SoulTalk, I might put words like these to their developing brokenness and repentance and abandonment, and invite them to pray: "God, we plead with you to restore our daughter to wholeness in Christ. But if that never happens, we declare today that the deepest longing of our hearts is to know and enjoy and reveal you to others. Free us in our brokenness to celebrate your receiving grace as we approach you, to depend on the Son's redeeming grace as we face our sin and move forward, and to become sensitive to the Spirit's rhythmic grace as we enter the battle for our daughter's soul."

The cost of discipleship is high. SoulTalk would consider that. I might say, "Your priority is not to put a stop to her promiscuity. Your desire for her to be good has been stronger than your desire to know God. You must see your sin as worse than your daughter's. Only then will you be humble enough for God's life to flow out of you and into her whether through discipline, discussion, or debate."

As I imagined myself having these conversations with my friends, I could sense an excitement: *I might become the Spirit's instrument to move these people toward deeper spiritual formation.* If that happened, God would receive glory, and my friends would become centered in Christ and begin to dance with the Trinity. I would experience joy, and their daughter might see what was going on and be drawn to God.

I thought about the possibilities. If these parents put first things first, they would provide their daughter with a strength she could not control and a love she could not destroy. The pressure she was feeling from her parents would be nudged aside and a new desire would emerge, prompted by the intersection of her humanness and God's Spirit. She wants love. The Spirit offers it. Combustion into worship could follow.

The Spirit is always moving. That's what the parents—and I—must believe. As they move toward their daughter with second-thing passion, exploring with friends what wise movement might look like, the Spirit will be moving. He will enter her now-puzzled soul ("What's gotten into my parents? They seem different") through the doorway of surprise ("That's not what I expected from them").

She may resist his voice. God grants us the dignity of choice. Coercion is not love. He is working to generate love in her soul, for God, for her parents, for the boys she misused by sleeping with them, for herself as a work of art in the making. She may say no to God. No parent controls that choice. But parents can pray. And in the mystery of sovereign movement, people, even hardened rebels, sometimes move toward God.

And that would be a source of great joy to her parents. But it would not be life. They already have that.

It might happen that way. It might not. The parents might

never leave the Old Way. Their daughter may never bring joy to her parents' hearts. We'll have to wait and see.

THE DANCE LESSONS OF SOULTALK

SoulTalk is a privilege. It has the power to change lives. It's the language God longs for us to speak, consisting of five dance lessons:

- *Think beneath* to see the battle.
- *Think vision* to see what could happen.
- *Think passion* to see what's in you that will get in the way.
- *Think story* to see inside the people you love.
- *Think movement* to enter the mystery of the Spirit's movement.

I want to do everything I can to help you to learn the language of SoulTalk. We all speak it a little, but too often the way a visitor from the United States to Spain reaches back into his memory of high school Spanish and stumbles through a few phrases. But I want to speak it well. And I want you to speak it well.

Read this book again. Discuss it with friends. Teach it in Sunday school or, if you have opportunity, from the pulpit.

Think about the metaphors of dancing with the Trinity, entering the soul's deepest battle, and listening to the Spirit to see where he's heading in someone's life. What do they mean? Talk about them with a friend, with your family, with your pastor or counselor.

Don't be discouraged. You can speak SoulTalk. The Spirit is in you, and SoulTalk is the language he speaks. And remember—it's the language God wants you to speak. It's the language God may use to revitalize the church and to introduce people all across the world to the New Way to live available only in Jesus.

I will close this book with a few thoughts on how, by God's grace, with Jesus' example, and in the Spirit's power, we can reverse the self-obsession that's destroying our world, corrupting our country, and weakening the church, and how we can instead move toward God-obsession.

Let me issue a call: Live the New Way of the Spirit. Abandon religion. Get on the spiritual journey. Learn the unforced rhythms of grace until you're dancing with the Trinity and entering the battle for the souls of people you love by speaking SoulTalk.

May God give us grace to learn the language he longs for us to speak.

Epilogue

Big Doors Swing on Small Hinges

W E MAY BE ON THE FRONT EDGE of a spiritual revolution. The Spirit speaks quietly, most often in the souls of unnoticed people, to do his mightiest work. Revolutions begin in coffee shops and living rooms, not in stadiums.

The foundation has been laid. People in the Christian church all over the world are awakening to the realization that three divine Persons are throwing a party, and they have invited us to know them, to party with them, and to live our lives on earth with their energy.

We are discovering the deep yearning in our soul to know our real Father. We feel a strange pull to follow a leader who is invisible to us, a Savior who demands absolute loyalty, who promises suffering if we follow him, and who sends us into mortal combat with no weapons we can see. And we actually believe a divine Person lives inside us, as surely as our human neighbor lives next-door.

We're waking up to the hope that we could know these three Persons, that they've made themselves available to be known better than we know anyone else, even a spouse of fifty years or a lifelong friend.

About a decade ago, I was sitting in a hot tub with a close friend who had less than a year to live. During that long soak under a clear night sky, we experienced a level of soul communion I've rarely known. He later told me that after I left he looked into the star-filled heavens and cried, "God, I know my friend better than I know you. That breaks my heart with desire, and I know it breaks your heart. I will pay any price to know you better."

A month before he died, he told me he could think of nothing he desired more than to be with the three Persons he knew best.

Several years later, I spent an evening with an elderly saint. The man lived in the presence of his heavenly Father. He had surrendered everything to follow his Lord and bore the scars of battle. His words flowed in gentle rhythm with the divine Spirit that filled his spirit. In three hours of conversation, mostly about my struggling journey, he said little.

But the fragrance of Christ filled the room. It was as strong as the aroma from a blooming bed of gardenias. When we parted and I returned to my hotel room, I fell to the floor and cried, "Holy Trinity, I will pay any price to know each of you the way that man does." That was one of the most transcendent moments of my life. And it happened because a man who knew God spoke SoulTalk to me.

The clearest evidence that we know our Father and love Jesus and hear the Spirit is not the size of our churches or the slickness of our events or the visible success we enjoy in life and ministry. The clearest evidence that we're dancing with the Trinity is the way we relate to others. It's the way we talk backed up by the way we live.

SelfTalk is cheap. SoulTalk is not. SoulTalk requires death to the self, the crucifixion of self-obsession, and the resurrection of God-obsession. Authentic SelfTalk ("I'll say whatever I want to say; I'll be true to me") is selfishness in the name of freedom. Religious SelfTalk ("Here's how to get God on your side. You can make good things happen") worships a false god of convenience and cooperation.

Only a few people speaking SoulTalk are needed to spread the fire.

SoulTalk is divine. It is a miracle of divine grace. It releases the power of God into the souls of people we love. We put God first. He works through us as he chooses. I know you've been hurt. *Enter the battle for the soul of the one who hurt you.* I know you want your spouse and your friend to treat you well. *Make that a second thing and enter the battle for their souls by treating them well.* I know you feel called to plant a church. *Be more concerned with whether your enjoyment of God is the energy behind your call rather than whether the church does well.*

When you do, supernatural power will flow out of your soul into the souls of others. Not everyone will respond, but many will. And you'll dance together. Transcendence will become more real. You'll relax in the Father's arms. You'll delight in the Messiah's love. And you'll dance even better to the Spirit's music.

Big doors swing on small hinges. Only a few people speaking SoulTalk are needed to spread the fire.

One elder can transform an elder board into a safe community where business is conducted among people who struggle well together. I know of an elder board that wants to write vision statements of what they see the Spirit doing in each other's soul.

One pastor can become a shepherd, a servant who doesn't care about titles or recognition, who leads with the power of a broken life that hungers for God and lives humbly in community, as one pilgrim among many. One broken pastor can transform a church, perhaps losing some members but lighting a fire under others.

One small group leader can listen to the Spirit more than manage the group process. The real battles going on in people's souls may slowly surface, and the group may creatively respond with Spirit-led SoulTalk.

One pew sitter can admit how desperately she longs to know God in ways she doesn't and how badly she wants to relate to others at church in ways that scare her out of her wits. It may take weeks; it may take years. It may divide before it unites. But one pew sitter who learns to speak SoulTalk ("Care to join me for lunch after church?") can create pockets of SoulTalking communities that will restore meaning to the word *church.*

I'm a chart kind of guy. If you're not, just glance at the chart on page 264. If you're like me, the chart might help. Reflect on each element. You'll recognize the five dance lessons I wrote about in this book.

Ask God to help you learn SoulTalk. Tell him you'll pay any price to know the Father, Son, and Spirit in a way that empowers you to speak the language they long for you to speak.

Pray that you'll recognize your next opportunity for SoulTalk. Don't follow the chart. Let it simply tune your ears to hear the music of heaven. Then dance.

Can you see it? Can you hear the music? Are you drawn to the rhythm? Can you feel the urge to dance?

The next time someone you love shares a struggle, lead with your ears. Say little. Listen for evidence of the Old Way. Discern where New Way energy is springing up and lifting the person into the presence of God.

Reflect on your motives. Trying to impress? Afraid you won't? Tell God you'd love to love. Then ask questions of your friend. Don't meddle. Don't pry. Don't push. Be curious and caring. Discuss what you see—fear, resentment, self-protection, hope, brokenness.

When you see movement, mention it with excitement. Celebrate. You're dancing with a person you love into the presence of God.

You've joined the revolution. You're speaking the language of divine love, the language God longs for all of us to speak. You're speaking SoulTalk. And you're bringing glory to God. There is no greater joy.

Welcome to kingdom living!

THE DANCE OF SOULTALK

Someone you love tells you about something going on in his/her life

↓

1. THINK BENEATH: Don't speak quickly. Think about the battle between religion and Christianity. Is this person more aware of his/her desire for blessings or desire for God?

↓

3. THINK PASSION: How are you right now self-obsessed? Feel it, confess it to God, and let brokenness put you in touch with your true desire to love this person.

← 2. THINK VISION: Reflect on how this person would be talking about his/her life if he/she wanted God more than his blessings. What would it mean for this person's life to not be wasted?

4. THINK STORY: Listen with transcendent curiosity to hear the hidden story of fear and shame and to hear shaping events that directed this person away from God in order to find life. Ask lots of questions. Be stingy with advice.

5. THINK MOVEMENT: Pay close attention to any movement toward brokenness. Then put words to repentance, encourage specific acts of trust, share your confidence in God, and celebrate release of the person's true self.

Notes

Chapter 2: We Need a New Way to Relate

1. C. S. Lewis, *The Weight of Glory* (1949; repr., New York: HarperCollins, 2001), 46.

Chapter 4: Want God More Than Anything Else

1. Peter Kreeft, *The Ants and the Angels* (Ann Arbor, Mich.: Servant Publications, 1994), 12–13.
2. Tim Burke, *Major League Dad* (Colorado Springs: Focus on the Family, 1999).

Chapter 6: Move In for a Closer Look

1. For a detailed discussion of the New Way versus the Old Way, see the author's book *The Pressure's Off* (Colorado Springs: Waterbrook, 2002).

Chapter 7: Go After the Very Best

1. C. S. Lewis, "First and Second Things," *God in the Dock* (1970; repr., Grand Rapids: Eerdmans, 2002), 280.
2. Alastair V. Campbell, quoted in Kenneth Leech, *Spirituality and Pastoral Care* (Cambridge, Mass.: Cowley Publications, 1989), 35.
3. Ibid., 51.
4. Saint Augustine, quoted in Brennan Manning, *The Rabbi's Heartbeat* (Colorado Springs: NavPress, 2003).

Chapter 9: Keep Looking Deep Inside

1. Quoted in Stephen F. Olford, *Heart-Cry for Revival* (Westwood, N.J.: Fleming H. Revell, 1962), 17.

Chapter 13: Listen to How a Story Is Told

1. Thomas Cahill, *How the Irish Saved Civilization* (New York: Doubleday, 1995), 39.
2. Ibid.
3. Ibid.

Chapter 15: Lead Others to a New Life in a New Land

1. André-Georges Malreaux, quoted in Thomas Cahill, *How the Irish Saved Civilization* (New York: Doubleday, 1995), 218.

Chapter 17: Enter the Mystery of Movement

1. For an extensive discussion of the cycle of spiritual formation, see the author's book *The Pressure's Off* (Colorado Springs: Waterbrook, 2002).